Plays for Holly Days

by Various Authors

Single copies of plays are sold for reading purposes only. The copying or duplicating of a play, or any part of play, by hand or by any other process, is an infringement of the copyright. Such infringement will be vigorously prosecuted.

Baker's Plays
7611 Sunset Blvd.
Los Angeles, CA 90042
bakersplays.com

NOTICE

This book is offered for sale at the price quoted only on the understanding that, if any additional copies of the whole or any part are necessary for its production, such additional copies will be purchased. The attention of all purchasers is directed to the following: this work is fully protected under the copyright laws of the United States of America, the British Commonwealth, including Canada, and all other countries of the Copyright Union. Violations of the Copyright Law are punishable by fine or imprisonment, or both. The copying or duplication of this work or any part of this work, by hand or by any process, is an infringement of the copyright and will be vigorously prosecuted.

This play may not be produced by amateurs or professionals for public or private performance without first submitting application for performing rights. Licensing fees are due on all performances whether for charity or gain, or whether admission is charged or not. Since performance of this play without the payment of the licensing fee renders anybody participating liable to severe penalties imposed by the law, anybody acting in this play should be sure, before doing so, that the licensing fee has been paid. Professional rights, reading rights, radio broadcasting, television and all mechanical rights, etc. are strictly reserved. Application for performing rights should be made directly to BAKER'S PLAYS.

No one shall commit or authorize any act or omission by which the copyright of, or the right to copyright, this play may be impaired. No one shall make any changes in this play for the purpose of production.

Publication of this play does not imply availability for performance. Both amateurs and professionals considering a production are strongly advised in their own interest to apply to Baker's Plays for written permission before starting rehearsals, advertising, or booking a theatre.

Whenever the play is produced, the author's name must be carried in all publicity, advertising and programs. Also, the following notice must appear on all printed programs, "Produced by special arrangement with Baker's Plays."

Licensing fees for PLAYS FOR HOLLY DAYS are based on a per performance rate and payable one week in advance of the production.

Please consult the Baker's Plays website at www.bakersplays.com or our current print catalogue for up to date licensing fee information.

Copyright © 1969 by Walter H. Baker Company
Made in U.S.A.
All rights reserved.

PLAYS FOR HOLLY DAYS
ISBN **978-0-87440-680-1**
#1195-B

CONTENTS

	Page
CHRISTMAS EVE BLUES *by Kurtz Gordon*	5
THE LADIES DISCOVER CHRISTMAS *by Anne Coulter Martens*	13
'TIS THE SEASON TO BE JOLLY *by Kurtz Gordon*	28
CHRISTMAS FOR CARLA *by Anne Coulter Martens*	39
THE MERRY-GO-ROUND GIFT *by Anne Coulter Martens*	54
CHRISTMAS TREES FOR SALE *by Dorothy C. Allan*	67
MEET MR. C. *by Anne Coulter Martens*	93

CHRISTMAS EVE BLUES

CHARACTERS

HELEN.
GEORGE, *her husband.*
TED, *their son.*

TIME: Christmas Eve.
SCENE: Kitchen (merely a table and two chairs needed).

(*As the curtain rises, the stage is in darkness. A door off* R. *opens and closes with a loud bang.*)

HELEN (*off* R.). Quiet, George! You'll wake up the boys. And heaven knows they get up early enough as it is on Christmas morning.

(*A light switch clicks off* R. *and a circle of light floods the kitchen table and two chairs at* C. *One chair faces* C. *back of table, the other is to the* L. *of it.* HELEN *and* GEORGE *enter* R. *They are both in casual attire and wear winter jackets.*)

GEORGE. What time is it?
HELEN. It's after eleven and we were only going over to the Joneses' for a short one.
GEORGE (*taking off his jacket*). Well, you just can't accept a neighbor's Christmas Eve cheer, gulp it down and say good night.

HELEN (*removing her jacket*). I knew all along we should have declined with thanks. You remember what happened over there last Christmas Eve, don't you?

GEORGE (*his hand to his forehead*). Don't remind me! We didn't get home until two in the morning and I had that damn toy to assemble before going to bed.

HELEN. Well, you've got another one of those damn toys to assemble tonight for Tommy.

GEORGE (*throwing his jacket over kitchen chair*). I don't think this one will take too long to assemble. The directions read fairly simple.

HELEN (*dropping her jacket on top of George's*). That's what you said last year and you know you're about as mechanically inclined as a peeled banana.

GEORGE (*resenting her remark*). That's right, Helen, rub it in! Merry Christmas!

HELEN (*soothing him with a smile*). You know what I mean, honey. It always makes you irritable when things don't fall right in place for you.

GEORGE. Well, I studied those instructions carefully late last night while you were putting the final touches to the Christmas tree and I bet, right now, I could put the thing together blindfolded.

HELEN. Say, that's not a bad idea, George. Let's try it this year. You bring out the toy and I'll make up a blindfold and you'll have the toy assembled in a (*snaps her fingers*) one-two-three!

GEORGE (*sarcastically*). Very funny!

HELEN (*picks up the jackets*). You get the box and I'll hang up these jackets.

GEORGE. Is the box still upstairs in our bedroom?

HELEN. No, I brought it downstairs just before

CHRISTMAS EVE BLUES

we left for the Joneses' and put it in the closet under the stairs.

GEORGE. Okay! (*He exits* L. *and* HELEN *exits* R. *In a few seconds you hear* GEORGE *rattling a doorknob off* L. *He is impatient and yells off* L.) What did you do, lock it?

HELEN (*entering* R.). What did you say, George?

GEORGE (*loudly off* L.). I asked you if you locked the door?

HELEN (*crossing to* L.). Not so loud, George, you'll wake up the boys!

GEORGE (*off* L.). Well, I can't open the door to the closet.

HELEN. It's not locked.

(GEORGE *rattles the doorknob again.*)

GEORGE (*off* L.). It's jammed or something!

HELEN. Which way are you turning that knob?

GEORGE (*off* L.). To the right.

HELEN. No wonder it doesn't open. You turn it to the left.

GEORGE (*off* L.). Since when?

HELEN. Since always! Try turning it to the left. (*She waits briefly then calls to him.*) Did it open?

GEORGE (*off* L.). Yea, I got it! (HELEN *starts back to the table.* GEORGE *yells again.*) Where did you hide it?

HELEN (*crossing to* L. *again*). I shoved it in the corner up against the stairs. (*A loud bump off* L.)

GEORGE (*off* L.). OUCH!

HELEN (*calling to him*). What happened?

GEORGE (*off* L.). I bumped my head on the stairs!

HELEN. GOOD! Now maybe you'll do as I asked months ago and put a light in that closet.

GEORGE (*off* L.). Very funny! How often do we use it?

HELEN. Well, often enough to get your head bumped! . . . Did you find it?

GEORGE (*off* L.). Yea, I got it! (HELEN *returns to the table.* GEORGE *enters* L. *with a cardboard box and rubbing his forehead. He crosses to* C. *and sets the box on the table.*) I'll need a screwdriver.

HELEN. I'll get it. (*Crosses to* R. *and exits.* GEORGE *takes out the parts to be assembled and lays them out in front of him on the table. He is very smug and pleased with himself.*) I'll show her this time! (*Sits on chair facing audience and picks up two of the parts.*) Now these two go together— I think! HELEN *enters* R. *with the screwdriver, crosses to table and sits on the other chair. Handing the screwdriver to* GEORGE.) Having trouble?

GEORGE. No, I'm not having trouble. (*Looks around the table then tries to shake something out of the box.*)

HELEN. Lose something?

GEORGE. The instruction sheet. Did you see it?

HELEN. You were the last one to have it. What did you do with it?

GEORGE (*very definitely*). I put it in the box.

HELEN. Then it's still there.

(GEORGE *shakes the box again; nothing comes out.*)

GEORGE. See? It's not there!

HELEN. Let me have that box. (GEORGE *hands it to* HELEN.)

CHRISTMAS EVE BLUES 9

GEORGE. Okay, big brain! You find it! (HELEN *takes the box, dives into the opening with her hand and brings out the instruction sheet and casually hands it to him.*)

HELEN. How's that?

GEORGE (*takes it gingerly from her*). It got stuck in there, that's why. (*Opens up the sheet, lays it flat on the table and reads from the instructions.*) Part A joins part B. (*Looks over the parts and selects two and tries to make them join. They won't connect. He tries to force them.*)

HELEN. Be careful, you'll break it!

GEORGE. Who's doing this, you or ME?

HELEN. From where I'm sitting, you're doing nothing that looks right. (*Pulls the instruction sheet toward her, scans it, then points to one of the parts in his hand.*) That's not part A, that's part C. (*Looks down at table and picks up another part and shows it to him.*) This is part A. (GEORGE *snatches it out of her hand.*)

GEORGE (*annoyed*). Okay, Lady Einstein! (*Drops the rejected part and tries to assemble the other two. They are not compatible. He gives* HELEN *a scathing look.*) Believe me, a Santa Claus helper, you are NOT!

HELEN. And for a good reason. According to the diagram here on the instruction sheet, that's NOT part B you have there in your hand, it's part D.

GEORGE (*irritated*). Why don't you find something else to do and leave me alone?

HELEN. Like what?

GEORGE (*beginning to seethe*). Set fire to the Christmas tree, for all I care!

HELEN (*rising from chair and standing at his*

side). With your brilliant aptitude, you'll be sitting in that chair come next Christmas Eve.

GEORGE (*sarcastically*). Still the comic, aren't you?

HELEN (*with a wave of her hand*). All right! All right! You do it your way!

GEORGE. Thanks! Get lost! (*He resumes his task.* HELEN *leans over his shoulder to watch.* GEORGE, *looking up at her and glaring.*) STOP breathing DOWN my neck!

(TED, *their ten-year-old son, enters quietly from* L. *He is dressed in pajamas and slippers. He walks silently and slowly over to the table and stops next to* HELEN.)

HELEN. There you go again, George, getting irritable!

GEORGE (*raising his voice*). I'm not IRRITABLE!

HELEN. Then it's a darn good imitation!

(TED *leans over the table to look at the unassembled toy.* HELEN *sees him out of the corner of her eye. She reacts with a loud exclamation and tries to cover the parts with her arms.*)

GEORGE. What's the matter with you? Have you gone NUTS! (HELEN *looks at* GEORGE *but is pointing to* TED. GEORGE *discovers him.*) What are you doing down here?

TED. I'm thirsty. I want a Coke. (HELEN *looks at him and is relieved.*)

HELEN. Oh, it's you, Ted. I thought it was Tommy.

CHRISTMAS EVE BLUES

TED. Are you having trouble again, Dad?

GEORGE. Now don't you start! Get your Coke and go back to bed.

HELEN. I'll get it for you, Ted. (*Exits off* R.)

(TED *stands and watches* GEORGE *as he fumbles with the parts.*)

TED. It's a good thing, Dad, you don't work on an assembly line.

GEORGE. What's that supposed to mean?

TED. You haven't got the aptitude.

GEORGE (*glaring at* TED). First it was your mother and now it's YOU! No coaching from the side-lines, understand? (TED *nods in assent.*) GOOD! (*Goes back to the toy, tries to fit two other parts together. They won't join.*)

TED. That's not the way it looks on the diagram, Dad.

GEORGE. QUIET!

TED. Sorry. (GEORGE *tries again to fit the parts together. He doesn't succeed.*) It will never work that way, Dad. (GEORGE *looks up at* TED, *gives him a scornful glance, drops one of the parts, picks up another then sheepishly looks up at* TED *for approval.* TED *shakes his head slowly.* GEORGE *drops that part and picks up another. Again he looks up at* TED *for sanction.* TED *vigorously shakes his head.*)

GEORGE (*capitulating*). Okay, Genius! You're so smart, you try it! (GEORGE *rises from the chair in utter dejection.*) Right now, what I need is a good COLD beer! (*Exits off* R.)

(TED *sits on the chair* GEORGE *vacated, looks*

over the parts on the table, consults the diagram on the instruction sheet, then begins to assemble the toy rapidly and with no difficulties at all.)

BLACKOUT

THE LADIES DISCOVER CHRISTMAS
(An All-Woman Play)

CHARACTERS

CARRIE, *who decorates.*
ADELE, *who prints.*
BLANCHE, *who sews.*
JAN, *a new bride.*
ELAINE }
RHODA } *who take a survey.*

SCENE: Family room in Carrie's home.
TIME: A few days before Christmas.

NOTE

This play may be given with very little rehearsal. Each of the women may have her part near her as she works. RHODA and ELAINE may read their parts from their notebooks. The cast may be enlarged by dividing the lines and adding to the Fair activities.

(SCENE: *Carrie's family room which has been partially cleared of other furniture to give the ladies room to work. There are a couple of easy chairs, an end table and lamp. A sofa may be added, if desired. Two card tables have been set up with a straight chair at each. Drapes may be used as background. An exit*, L., *leads to other rooms, one*, R., *leads outside.*)

(AT RISE OF CURTAIN: CARRIE, ADELE, BLANCHE and JAN *are busy with preparations for the Christmas Fair. They may be of any age, but* JAN *should be a little younger. She is at a card table taking cookies from a large box and putting them into smaller Christmas boxes.* CARRIE *is kneeling on a cushion* D. C. *Newspapers are spread all around her and on the papers are small branches of evergreens and pine cones which she is spraying with a can of gold paint.* ADELE *is at the other card table putting the last touches on a large Christmas poster.* BLANCHE *sits in an easy chair sewing on a doll's dress. The doll is on the end table beside her. All of these activities may be almost completed.*)

ADELE (*as she works*). Darn! Paint on my arm again.

BLANCHE. You're getting more on yourself than on that poster.

CARRIE. I've sprayed both my hands gold.

BLANCHE. Want to change jobs with me and finish making this doll's dress?

ADELE. I'd sew my fingers together.

CARRIE. I promised I'd spray these evergreens in time for the Christmas Fair and I'll stick with it . . . if my poor knees hold out. How are you doing with the cookies, Jan? (*Raises the spray can without thinking.*)

JAN (*moving away quickly*). Don't spray *me!* (*As* CARRIE *lowers the can.*) Almost done. And then I simply have to leave and get some shopping done.

THE LADIES DISCOVER CHRISTMAS 15

ADELE. Only one more week. It hardly seems possible.

BLANCHE. Don't we say that every year?

CARRIE. Our club should hold this Fair *early* in December.

ADELE. Don't we say that every year? (*They laugh.*)

(*The doorbell rings.*)

CARRIE. Will one of you please answer the door out of respect for my aching knees?

JAN. Sure, I will. (*Goes* R.)

CARRIE. Probably some kid selling something. Candy, Christmas cards . . .

JAN. I haven't even bought mine yet. (*Goes out* R.)

ADELE. I thought I'd have time to make my own and now it's too late.

BLANCHE. You say *that* every year, too.

ADELE. I know. But Jan's a new bride, you'd think she'd be better organized.

CARRIE. We've had more years of experience . . . are *we* organized? (*They laugh cheerfully.* JAN *comes in with* ELAINE *and* RHODA, *women of any age.*)

JAN. Ladies, I thought you'd like to talk to Elaine Foster and Rhoda Bennett. They'll tell you why they're here.

ELAINE. We don't want to intrude, we can see you're all busy . . .

RHODA. But this will take only a few minutes of your time.

CARRIE (*warily*). Not magazines? I'm oversubscribed already.

ELAINE. No, not magazines. We're from the Gilman Research Center and we're doing a little survey about people's reactions to Christmas.

RHODA. You might call it a Christmas poll.

JAN. Sounds interesting.

ELAINE. Will you spare us a little time? It's all right if you go on working.

CARRIE. Why, I guess so.

ADELE. All right with me.

ELAINE. My partner, Rhoda, will go next door, and then return here later.

BLANCHE. If that's the way it's done.

RHODA. 'Bye for now. (*Goes out* R.)

ELAINE. Now, then . . . (*Takes out a pen and a pad.*)

CARRIE. Do sit down.

ELAINE (*sitting in the other easy chair*). I'm getting a little tired from walking up and down streets and ringing doorbells.

ADELE. You ask questions?

ELAINE. Just one question, and please think carefully before you answer it. In the language of today, "What bugs you about Christmas?"

(*The ladies laugh.*)

BLANCHE. If that isn't the most ridiculous question!

CARRIE. We all love Christmas.

ELAINE. That's the answer I usually get . . . at first.

JAN. This is my first Christmas as a wife and I'm trying to have everything just right.

ELAINE. Sure there isn't some little thing that

THE LADIES DISCOVER CHRISTMAS 17

bugs you? A lot of people are becoming annoyed with some aspects of the Christmas season.

CARRIE. Not me. I think it's great.

ADELE. Nothing like it.

BLANCHE. Best time of the year.

JAN. Oh, yes, the very best.

ELAINE. Everything's perfect? Think a minute, ladies.

CARRIE (*after a pause*). Well . . . maybe I'm just getting older, but there are such crowds in the stores.

ADELE. Worse every year.

ELAINE. As if people leave Christmas shopping to the very last minute.

JAN. Like me, and I did have such good intentions.

ELAINE (*writing*). Crowds.

ADELE. Prices, too. They jump sky-high just because an article has a red bow on it.

BLANCHE. Or comes in a fancy box.

CARRIE. People get carried away and just spend, spend, spend, even when they can't afford to.

JAN. Phil says we'll have to work out a budget.

ADELE (*to* JAN). My advice to you is, cut your list way down.

BLANCHE. January bills are an awful headache!

JAN. But there are always so many little extras . . .

CARRIE. Ask yourself are they really necessary?

ELAINE. M'm. (*Writing.*) High prices, unnecessary extras. Anything else?

CARRIE. Well, this Christmas Fair, for instance. I started out by volunteering to make some cookies, just as you did, Jan. And the next year I was chairman of a committee, and this year I'm in charge of the whole deal!

ADELE. I got stuck with it once. Never again!

BLANCHE. You learn to be wary.

CARRIE. If I were you, Jan, I'd steer clear of it next year, or you may be the patsy!

JAN. I didn't realize.

CARRIE. Show the least bit of interest, and you get all the work.

ELAINE (*writing*). Too many outside activities.

BLANCHE. Especially when we have so much to do at home. My children only half help with the tree, and as for Howard, I have to nag, nag, nag for a week to get him to put up the outdoor lights.

JAN. I have them on my shopping list, outdoor lights.

BLANCHE. Last year Howard claimed he sprained his back. And on that icy day before Christmas, there I was, up on a stepladder, putting them up myself! My fingers were so cold that when the hammer hit them I didn't even feel it.

JAN. Phil did promise he'd put ours up.

CARRIE. They'll promise you anything, especially when they're first married.

ADELE. Isn't that the truth!

BLANCHE. But don't be surprised if he comes home late from the office Christmas party, and *you* have to do it!

JAN (*uncertainly*). Maybe I'd better not buy any outdoor lights.

BLANCHE. Take my advice and skip it.

ELAINE (*writing*). Trouble with outdoor lights.

ADELE. While we're on the subject of what bugs us, I'd say . . . Christmas cards.

THE LADIES DISCOVER CHRISTMAS

CARRIE. Do you send many?

ADELE. Too many! And Arthur doesn't like the printed kind. I must sign every one. Have you any idea how long it takes to sign over two hundred Christmas cards?

BLANCHE. Not to mention putting them in envelopes and putting on stamps and seals.

JAN. I've been trying to decide on our list.

ADELE. Don't even start one!

BLANCHE. Really, what good are they, anyway?

CARRIE. You just throw them all away after Christmas.

JAN (*uncertainly*). I guess I won't buy any.

ADELE. Not that they aren't pretty, but after all . . .

JAN. Yes, I see what you mean.

ELAINE (*writing*). Christmas cards.

CARRIE. It bugs *me* to see a Santa Claus on every street corner and in every department store. What are children going to think?

BLANCHE. I heard of a beard-pulling incident that was disastrous.

ADELE. Children are naturally inquisitive.

CARRIE. If I see one more of those scrawny, bearded characters standing beside a booth, ringing a bell for donations, I'll . . .

BLANCHE. You'll what?

CARRIE. If at the same time a record is playing "Jingle Bells," I think I'll scream!

ADELE. We can't give to every organization that hires a Santa Claus.

BLANCHE. Charity does begin at home.

JAN. It *is* overdone. I'll pass them right by.

ELAINE (*writing*). Too many Santa Clauses. Anything else, ladies?

CARRIE. Goodness, you must have quite a list.

ELAINE. Sizable.

CARRIE. My knees are so stiff I just have to get up. (*Rises, taking the straight chair which* JAN *is not using.*) A relief to sit down.

ELAINE. If there isn't anything more, I'll be on my way.

ADELE. I didn't realize there were so many things that really bother us.

ELAINE. People usually don't, until they stop and think. Thank you, ladies, for your time. (*Gets up.*) Good-bye. (*As they call "good-byes" she goes out* R.)

CARRIE. I've reached a point where I don't care if these evergreens are sprayed or not.

ADELE. I've spent too much time on this poster. Why always *me?*

BLANCHE. I never did care for sewing. Oh, now I've broken my thread!

JAN. My mind has changed about a lot of things, and I still have shopping to do.

CARRIE. The time for you to set a precedent is right now.

ADELE. Don't let Christmas become too much for you.

JAN. I'll cut it down, omit, make it simpler.

BLANCHE. And more sensible.

CARRIE. That's what we all should do, have a sensible Christmas.

ADELE. You know, I'm rather glad that survey woman came.

BLANCHE. It makes me realize I've let myself get

THE LADIES DISCOVER CHRISTMAS

carried away. (*To* JAN.) Don't let it happen to you!

JAN. Definitely not. (*Closes a box of cookies, sighs.*) I seem to have lost any desire to rush out and join the crowds.

CARRIE. Shoving and pushing and stepping on your toes.

ADELE. Jamming into the elevator when there isn't any more room.

BLANCHE. Arms full of packages that poke you in the eye.

CARRIE. And when you do get up to a store counter, they're always out of whatever size or color you want.

ADELE. So you have to go through the same thing in the next store.

BLANCHE. I begin to wonder if it's worth all the effort.

(JAN *sighs.*)

CARRIE. Something the matter, Jan?
JAN. No. Oh, no.
ADELE. Frankly, I don't have my old enthusiasm for Christmas.
BLANCHE. Neither do I, though it's hard to say just why.
JAN. I always enjoyed it so much.
CARRIE. So did we all . . . once.
ADELE. But now it's just a lot of fuss over . . . what?
BLANCHE. The day after New Year's we take the tree down, anyway. And then it's nag, nag, nag to get Howard to take down the outdoor lights.

CARRIE. What bugs me about Christmas? Practically everything! (*The doorbell rings.*) I'll get it. (*Goes out* R.)

ADELE. Poor Carrie's overtired.

BLANCHE. Aren't we all?

JAN. The way I feel now, I'll be glad when Christmas is over.

(CARRIE *comes in* R. *with* RHODA.)

CARRIE. It's the other survey questioner.

RHODA. I told you I'd be back.

CARRIE. But we've already answered your teammate's question.

RHODA (*cheerfully*). Mine is a different question. (*Sits down and takes out a pad and pen.*) "What pleases you about Christmas?"

CARRIE. Pleases?

ADELE. You mean, what do we like about it?

RHODA. Exactly.

JAN. We've all decided to omit the fuss and have a sensible Christmas.

RHODA. Not even a Christmas tree?

CARRIE. Oh, we'll have to have a Christmas tree. The children count on it.

ADELE. Everybody in my family likes a big one.

BLANCHE. One thing Howard *will* do. He'll climb up and put the star at the very top.

CARRIE. When ours is decorated, we turn out all the other lights and turn on the tree lights.

ADELE. Every year it makes me catch my breath.

BLANCHE. As if something magic has suddenly happened.

THE LADIES DISCOVER CHRISTMAS 23

JAN. Then Phil and I are going to buy a big tree!

RHODA. M'm. You all like Christmas trees. Anything else?

ADELE. Come to think of it, cards are a colorful decoration if you know what to do with them. I tape mine to red ribbons and hang them in a doorway.

BLANCHE. We display ours on a wall ledge in our family room.

CARRIE. Mine, I keep in a little pile on a table so I can keep looking through them.

ADELE. After Christmas I read all the messages again. I have friends living all over the country, people I used to know and may never see again. But they write me little personal messages, telling how things are going for them. And, you know, it's rather nice.

BLANCHE. A way of keeping in touch.

CARRIE. Remembering people you used to know and still do know when the card comes.

ADELE. Sure, I complain about how many I have to send. But I must admit it pleases me to get just as many.

BLANCHE. As if a friend is saying hello to you.

CARRIE. And wishing you well.

ADELE. Jan, I guess I was wrong in advising you not to send Christmas cards.

JAN. Phil and I will have a long, long list!

RHODA (*writing*). Christmas cards. And?

BLANCHE. Well . . . even though I have to nag Howard to put up the outdoor lights, they're a joy to look at once they're up.

ADELE. We try to have a different design every year.

CARRIE. Last year our lawn lighting won first prize.

BLANCHE. They're trouble, sure. But I'd hate to have the front of our house dark at Christmastime.

JAN. Then you think I should put outdoor lights on my Christmas list?

BLANCHE. By all means. Phil will help you.

JAN. Oh, I'm sure he will.

RHODA (*writing*). Outdoor lighting. Go on, ladies.

CARRIE. Let me think. Prices *are* pretty high. But if you're ever going to splurge on a gift, then Christmas is the time.

BLANCHE. It's almost as if we're glad to spend more.

ADELE. We've coped with January bills before. I guess it's just part of Christmas.

CARRIE. The truth is, we enjoy giving nice gifts. (*To* JAN.) Pay no attention to what I told you about cutting your list down.

JAN. Now I feel better about it.

RHODA (*writing*). Gift giving. Everyone enjoys it.

CARRIE. Even the street-corner Santas. It's hard to imagine a Christmas without them.

ADELE. I always give something, no matter what the charity.

BLANCHE. Even the Santas need a pay check.

CARRIE. And lots of charities are worth while. Like the Children's Home where we give the money we raise from our Christmas Fair.

ADELE. We do work hard, especially when we're so busy with other things. . . .

BLANCHE. But it gives us a good feeling when we present them with a nice big check.

THE LADIES DISCOVER CHRISTMAS 25

JAN. Maybe I didn't waste my time baking all these cookies.

BLANCHE. Of course you didn't.

CARRIE. When the time comes that you're asked to be in charge of the Fair, you'll do it just as the rest of us did.

RHODA (*writing*). Christmas charities, approved. More?

CARRIE. I don't like crowds. But if they're shopping at the last minute, so am I.

ADELE. It's no fun to have all your gifts bought and wrapped way ahead of time.

BLANCHE. Part of the excitement is hurry, hurry, hurry to get just what you want.

CARRIE. And there's something about Christmas crowds. They're *nicer* than at any other time of the year.

ADELE. Some people even hold the store door open for you.

BLANCHE. And apologize if they bump into you.

CARRIE. I might even miss hearing "Jingle Bells."

ADELE. It makes you walk faster, feel happier. . . .

BLANCHE. You sort of sing inside.

ADELE. All Christmas music does that.

BLANCHE. I still get a lump in my throat when I hear "Silent Night."

JAN (*happily*). I'll buy an album of Christmas music for Phil and me!

CARRIE. Yes, Jan, it's a must.

RHODA (*writing*). Christmas music. Anything else?

CARRIE. I think we've about covered it all. Christmas means rush, and spend and decorate, wrap and mail and a dozen other things. But there's something about the day, when it finally comes, that makes it all worth while.

ADELE. A sort of hush falls over you . . .

BLANCHE. A feeling of peace . . .

JAN. Because everything you've done, you've done out of love. Oh, Christmas is wonderful, isn't it?

CARRIE. Yes, Jan, it really is.

RHODA (*rising*). Ladies, you've given me my answer. (*The doorbell rings.*) Come in! My partner returning.

(ELAINE *comes in* R.)

ELAINE. Finished?

RHODA. Yes.

ELAINE. How did the survey come out?

RHODA. Exactly the same way it does in every place we visit. Your question makes them complain. My question makes them appreciate.

ELAINE. Everybody loves Christmas?

CARRIE. We do, indeed!

RHODA. Happy holiday! (*She and* ELAINE *go out* R. *as the others call "Merry Christmas!" after them.*)

CARRIE. Let's hurry and finish our work. (*Gets down on her knees and sprays some evergreens.*)

ADELE (*holding up the poster which advertises the Fair and is decorated with sprays of holly*). Not bad, is it?

BLANCHE (*who has slipped the dress on the doll*). Isn't she adorable?

JAN. Phil and I are going to have the best Christmas ever! (*Nibbles on a cookie from the large box.*)

CARRIE. Hey, don't eat up the profits! (*Starts to sing "Jingle Bells" and they all join in.*)

CURTAIN

'TIS THE SEASON TO BE JOLLY

CHARACTERS

MARY
JOE
HILDA
JEAN } *employees.*
FRED
BILL
PEGGY
MR. WORRIMANN, *department head.*
THELMA, *his secretary.*
MR. MERRYWEATHER, *the new regional boss.*

SCENE: A cleared office desk at a Christmas party.

(*A bright, cheery, paper tablecloth covers the top of the desk. The audience [employees and their guests] sit casually at a respectful distance to watch the "Happening." When the audience has quieted down, if possible, MARY breaks the silence [?] with a warning command.*)

MARY. Careful with that punch bowl, Joe! Don't drop it!

JOE (*enters the scene carrying a large punch bowl with a ladle to the desk*). I'm as steady and sober as a judge.

(MARY *enters scene and follows* JOE *to the desk.*)

Mary. They don't come packaged that way around Christmastime. (*Then hurrying to the desk.*) Put it down carefully, Joe. Remember we rented it, we didn't borrow it, and we're responsible if it's broken. (*With noticeable difficulty,* Joe *manages to set the punch bowl on the desk.*)

Joe. Okay, Calamity Mary! There it is all in one piece.

Mary (*with a sigh of relief*). Thank heavens! It's still the age of miracles.

Joe. What do you mean, miracles?

Mary. I heard about that big, substantial lunch you had today. Three olives in you know what?

Joe (*with a careless gesture of his hand*). Just a runner-up for the big event.

Mary. You'd better watch that stuff. Our regional boss is scheduled to honor us at our Christmas party.

Joe. Oh, you mean old man Merryweather?

Mary. I understand he's not old. As a matter of fact, we don't actually know how old he is.

Joe. My mental computer registers an old fogy.

Mary. My advice to you is take a walk outside and spin the wheels in your head. It's essential that we all make an impression while Mr. Merryweather is here.

Joe. Oh, I will, I will! Just leave it to me.

Mary. That's what bothers me. I'm speaking of something on the favorable side.

(Hilda *and* Jean *enter the scene.* Hilda *carries a tray of sandwiches and* Jean *a tray with cans of fruit juices, canned fruits, bottle of ginger ale, etc., to make a punch. They set the trays on the desk.*)

JEAN. Well, here's the liquid foundation. (*Looks on top of the desk.*) Where's the ice?

HILDA. Fred's bringing it.

JEAN. And the glasses?

HILDA. Peggy and Bill are taking care of those. Peggy thought they should be given a rinse.

(FRED *comes into the scene with a bucket of ice cubes.*)

FRED. Here's the ice. (*Sets it on the desk.*)

JEAN. What do we put in first? The ice or the juice?

JOE. Ice first, gin second, juice last.

MARY (*very definite*). No liquor! Orders from the forward echelon.

FRED. No spike? No stick?

MARY (*emphatically*). No NOTHING!

HILDA. Who's giving this party, Carrie Nation?

MARY. Orders from our boss, Mr. Worrimann. He doesn't know if Mr. Merryweather would approve.

FRED. Well, why doesn't he find out?

MARY. That's exactly what he's trying to do now. He's been on the phone for the last half hour and still no clearance.

JEAN. Well, let's get this brew stirring. . . . What shall I put in first?

JOE. Start with the ice. I have the most beautiful bottle of punch flavoring in the bottom drawer of my desk just made to order for this kind of concoction. I'll be right back, don't go away! (*Walks out of scene.* MARY *chases after him.*)

MARY. Joe! Don't you dare!

'TIS THE SEASON TO BE JOLLY

FRED (*to the others*). What good is a Christmas punch if it hasn't got a spike in it?

JEAN. Might just as well drink a Sunday School soda.

HILDA. Or have a seance without a spirit.

(BILL *and* PEGGY *enter the scene carrying two more trays.* BILL *is carrying the glasses and* PEGGY *has plates of cold cuts, cheese, pickles, crackers, etc., with her handbag dangling from her arm. They join the group and set their trays on the desk.*)

BILL (*looking into the punch bowl*). Hey? How's about getting this cauldron going?

JEAN. That's what I say. Put in the ice, Fred.

FRED. Right! (*Dumps ice cubes in the punch bowl.*)

JEAN (*adding the fruit juices*). Here goes the giggle water without the giggle.

BILL (*snapping his fingers*). Which reminds me. There's an urgent matter that needs my immediate attention in the bottom drawer of my desk. Be back in a jiffy. (*Leaves the scene.*)

HILDA (*calling to him*). Bring it back alive!

FRED. What's all this big noise about Mr. Merryweather?

JEAN. He's some big shot in the organization and the boss has never met him. He insists that we all make a good impression.

FRED. But this is an office Christmas party. We don't make good impressions. We practically shatter the ones we've already made.

JEAN. You know how the boss is. Lives up to his

name in every way. Worries about everything. (*Stirs the punch.*)

HILDA. When there's nothing for him to worry about, he starts worrying about why he's not worrying.

JEAN. Let's dump the fruit in here next. (*Starts to add the canned fruit.*)

PEGGY. Not so heavy with the garbage, Jean. It will look like a bowl of Jello.

JEAN. (*holding off*). Is that enough?

PEGGY. Plenty.

JEAN (*picking up bottle of ginger ale*). How much of this ginger ale shall I add?

PEGGY. Go light on that, too. (*Open her handbag and brings out a pint bottle.*) This is what should go in there next. (*Unscrews cap from bottle.*)

FRED. What is it?

PEGGY. A sample of my Dad's homemade applejack.

HILDA. Good! Gurgle it in.

JEAN. Do we dare, without Mr. Worrimann's consent?

PEGGY. What he doesn't know, he can't worry about.

JEAN. Let's take a vote.

FRED. I have a better idea. How about flipping a coin?

HILDA. I'll buy that. (FRED *brings out a coin.*)

FRED. All agree? (*They all consent.*) Heads we do it and tails we don't. (*Flips the coin to the palm of his hand. They all watch.*) HEADS! See? (*He shows it to them.*)

PEGGY. Here goes! (*Empties contents of bottle into the punch bowl while* JEAN *stirs.*)

'TIS THE SEASON TO BE JOLLY

JEAN (*imitating a witch's voice*).
> Double, double toil and trouble
> Fire burn and cauldron bubble.

HILDA. Let me look at that coin, Fred.

FRED. Why?

HILDA. I suddenly recall your flipping this coin before.

FRED (*with a satisfied grin*). Okay! (*Hands it to her.* HILDA *inspects both sides.*)

HILDA (*holding out coin to the others*). Look! We've been tooken! This coin has two heads. (*They all look at it.*)

PEGGY (*in pretended anger*). Curse you, Jack Dalton!

JEAN. What a dirty, delicious, underhanded trick!

FRED (*with bowed head in shame*). Forgive me. Gambling is my weakness and I'm a poor loser.

HILDA (*returning the coin to him*). Don't ever reform if this is the way you lose.

PEGGY. Since we're all accessory after the fact, I'd better hide the evidence. (*Screws cap on bottle and returns it to her handbag.* JOE *enters the scene with a fifth of gin,* MARY *following at his heels.*)

MARY (*admonishing him*). Joe, if you dare, I swear I'll tell Mr. Worrimann.

JOE (*holding up bottle*). Let's add a little spirit to the party.

(BILL *enters the scene with another bottle.*)

BILL (*over to desk*). Here's something that will give it body and flavor.

FRED. Don't tell me what it is, just put it in.

BILL (*holding up bottle*). Spoken like a man!

MR. WORRIMANN (*shouting off scene*). STOP! (*Rushes to the desk.*) No liquor! We haven't got clearance yet. My secretary's still on the phone. We expect a definite answer soon.

MARY. Why, Mr. Worrimann, we wouldn't think of acting without your consent. (*Turns to the others.*) Would we?

THE OTHERS (*in unison*). Oh, no, Mr. Worrimann, NEVER!

MR. WORRIMANN (*with a deep sigh*). Oh, thank heavens for that! This situation puts me in a very precarious spot. You just don't realize the stress and strain I'm under. If Mr. Merryweather is an abstainer, a thing like this could prevent my promotion to a title in the official family.

THE OTHERS (*in unison*). Perish the thought, Mr. Worrimann!

JOE. Mr. Worrimann?

MR. WORRIMANN (*kindly*). Yes, Joe, what is it?

JOE (*holding up the bottle*). Just a thimbleful?

MR. WORRIMANN (*shouting*). NO!

(THELMA, *his secretary, enters the scene and crosses to him.*)

THELMA. Mr. Worrimann. (*He turns to her.*)

MR. WORRIMANN. Yes, Thelma.

THELMA. I think this can be regarded as a clearance, Mr. Worrimann. I received a phone call from Mr. Pedowitz, our executive vice president—

MR. WORRIMANN (*interrupting nervously*). Yes, yes. Come, come, Thelma, what did he say?

THELMA. Mr. Merryweather imbibed a cocktail at a dinner last night.

'TIS THE SEASON TO BE JOLLY 35

MR. WORRIMANN (*all smiles*). HE DID?

THELMA. That's the message Mr. Pedowitz gave me.

MR. WORRIMANN (*with hand to his forehead*). What a relief!

THELMA. Also, Mr. Worrimann—

MR. WORRIMANN (*on the defensive*). Now what?

THELMA. Mr. Merryweather left an hour ago and should arrive here any minute.

MR. WORRIMANN. Thank you, Thelma, thank you. Now get back to your desk. We'll let you know when everything is ready up here.

THELMA. Yes, Mr. Worrimann. (*Leaves the scene.* MR. WORRIMANN *turns to the others.*)

MR. WORRIMANN. Well, it looks like we have the green light.

JOE (*holding up bottle*). Okay to gurgle, Mr. Worrimann?

MR. WORRIMANN. Yes, Joe, but take it easy. Just enough spirits to give it taste.

JOE. Right! (*Starts pouring from the bottle.*)

MARY. Mr. Worrimann, when do you think we should start serving?

MR. WORRIMANN (*turning to her with his back to* BILL *and* JOE). Just as soon as Mr. Merryweather arrives I'll let you know.

(JOE *nudges* BILL *and nods to the punch bowl.* BILL *gives the Okay sign with his hand and starts pouring from his bottle.*)

MARY. Do you think we should make a pot of coffee?

FRED (*in disgust*). Coffee? UGH!

(THELMA *enters the scene hurriedly.*)

THELMA (*rushing to* MR. WORRIMANN). Mr. Worrimann! Mr. Worrimann!

MR. WORRIMANN. Yes, Thelma, what is it?

THELMA. Mr. Pedowitz called again and said he was just informed that the cocktail Mr. Merryweather had last evening was a Shirley Temple.

(MR. WORRIMANN *spins around excitedly to* JOE.)

MR. WORRIMANN. Stop the flow! STOP THE FLOW! NO SPIRITS! (JOE *and* BILL *stop pouring and shrug their shoulders.*)

JOE (*with a sad smile*). Too late, Mr. Worrimann.

MR. WORRIMANN (*in agony*). I'm finished! I'm ruined! Let me taste it! (JOE *takes a glass and ladles up a generous portion from the bowl and hands it to* MR. WORRIMANN.)

JOE. Here you are, Mr. Worrimann. (*He takes the glass and downs the contents in a few gulps.*)

MR. WORRIMANN. I can taste it! I can taste it!

(JOE *picks up a glass, dips it in the punch and sips it.*)

JOE. It's scarcely evident, Mr. Worriman. It's more like a flavor than a stimulant.

MR. WORRIMANN (*hopefully*). Really? Let me taste it again. (*Hands* JOE *his glass.* JOE *is very generous in filling it this time.*)

JOE (*handing glass to* MR. WORRIMANN). Here you are, Mr. Worrimann.

'TIS THE SEASON TO BE JOLLY

(MR. WORRIMAN *takes the glass and sips it this time instead of gulping.*)

MR. WORRIMANN (*after a few sips*). A little noticeable but not too bad, really.

(*A well-dressed, pompous, middle-aged man walks into the scene. It is* MR. MERRYWEATHER. *All are taken by surprise and root to the spot.* JOE *and* BILL *quickly hide the bottles behind their backs.*)

MR. MERRYWEATHER (*as he walks to* MR. WORRIMANN). Mr. Worrimann, I presume?
MR. WORRIMANN (*with importance*). Yes, sir, and who are you?
MR. MERRYWEATHER. I am Mr. Merryweather. I believe that I'm expected to honor your Christmas party.
MR. WORRIMANN (*nervous and excited*). Why, yes, yes, of course. Welcome, Mr. Merryweather. (*Instead of offering his free hand in greeting, he holds out the glass of punch.* MR. MERRYWEATHER *accepts it.*)
MR. MERRYWEATHER. Why, thank you, Mr. Worrimann. What a gracious and hospitable way to say, "Merry Christmas." (*Raises the glass to* MR. WORRIMANN.) To your good health, Mr. Worrimann. (*Then to the others.*) And to you all, "Greetings of the season." (*He drinks the punch, draining the glass.* MR. WORRIMANN *watches him, expecting the world to come to an abrupt end.* MR. MERRYWEATHER *smiles and looks down at the glass.*) Very refreshing! But I would say it needs a

little more character. (*He sets the glass on the desk, removes a flask from his inside pocket, unscrews the top and pours the contents slowly into the punch bowl, singing gaily:*) 'Tis the season to be jolly. Tra la-la, la-la, la-la!

(*The others pick up the tune, start filling their glasses and the party begins.*)

END OF HAPPENING

CHRISTMAS FOR CARLA
(An All-Girl Play)

CHARACTERS

CARLA, *a personal shopper.*
PATTY, *her secretary.*
SALLY, *a store clerk.*
GINNY, *a secretary.*
AUNT NELLIE, *a visitor.*

SCENE: Office of the personal shopper of a department store.

TIME: Afternoon. The day before Christmas.

(SCENE: *Office of the personal shopper in a department store. Drapes may be used as a background.* R. *there is an easy chair with a table for magazines and a lamp beside it. A desk and chair are* U. C. *On the desk are a telephone and various papers. Another desk and chair are near the wall* L. *On this desk are a small decorated Christmas tree and a typewriter. A door* R. *leads to a corridor.*)

(AT RISE OF CURTAIN: CARLA, *competent, fashionably dressed, and in her twenties, is seated at the desk* U. C. *writing as the telephone rings.*)

CARLA (*on the phone*). Baylor's Department Store. Carla Caldwell, personal shopper, speaking.

... Yes, Mrs. Marsh, your order was filled yesterday and should reach you by special messenger today. ... Thank you, we're glad to be of service. Good-bye. (*As she hangs up,* PATTY, *in her late teens, warm and enthusiastic, comes in. She has a small perfume box in her hand.* CARLA, *glancing at her watch.*) Patty, you asked for a ten-minute break and you've taken twenty.

PATTY. I'm sorry, Miss Caldwell. (*Puts box on* CARLA'S *desk.*) Mr. Davis sent back the perfume.

CARLA (*annoyed*). He what?

PATTY. I met his office boy at the elevator. He said Mr. Davis will call you about it.

CARLA. Oh, indeed?

PATTY. I don't know why he didn't like it.

CARLA. One of our best perfumes.

PATTY. "Siren," practically guaranteed to cure what's wrong with your love life.

CARLA. Don't be flippant, please.

PATTY (*going to the other desk*). My Eddie thinks I'm perfect the way I am.

CARLA. Get started on those letters. I want them to go out today.

PATTY. The day before Christmas? I didn't think they were so important.

CARLA (*coldly*). Office routine is always important and I see no reason to let Christmas interfere with it. (*The phone rings and she answers it.* PATTY *looks through some papers.*) Baylor's Department Store, Carla Caldwell, personal shopper, speaking. ... I selected a pale pink robe for you, Mrs. Andrews, and our truck will deliver it this afternoon. ... Thank you, we're glad to be of service. Good-bye. (*Hangs up.*)

CHRISTMAS FOR CARLA 41

PATTY. Why do people leave things to the last minute and then call the personal shopper?

CARLA (*writing on a pad*). Their reasons don't concern us.

PATTY. Wow, is that toy department out there crowded! A million mothers and their kids all trying to climb on poor Santa's lap.

CARLA (*dryly*). The mothers, too?

PATTY. You know what I mean. Squealing and yelling, and running and bumping into people, and everybody so happy you can just *feel* it.

CARLA (*busy*). M'm.

PATTY. I just love the toy department the day before Christmas.

CARLA. M'm.

PATTY. Sally, my girl friend, works at the doll counter.

CARLA. Have you forgotten you have letters to type?

PATTY (*sighing*). Can't I let them wait?

CARLA. Certainly not. I'm trying to make you an efficient secretary.

PATTY. I'm so excited about Christmas that I'd make a jumble of them.

CARLA. Try a little self-control.

PATTY. I keep thinking of all the things I have to do when I get home.

CARLA. M'm.

PATTY. My boy friend Eddie's coming over to help trim the tree. Did I ever tell you how nice he is?

CARLA. You did. I wish you'd stop chattering and get busy.

PATTY. All right. (*After a pause.*) I just want to ask you one question.

CARLA (*impatiently*). What is it?

PATTY. Can I get off a little early today? Eddie and I want to pick up my grandmother to spend Christmas with us.

CARLA. You must learn not to make plans that conflict with your working hours.

PATTY. You mean, I can't get off early?

CARLA. That's correct.

(PATTY *gives her a hurt look, then puts a piece of paper in her typewriter and begins to type. After a moment she stops.*)

PATTY. Miss Caldwell. (CARLA *looks up.*) It's okay. We can drive over for her in the evening.

CARLA. Good. (*Returns to her work.*)

PATTY. Are you going to spend Christmas with your folks?

CARLA (*after a pause*). Why do you ask?

PATTY. I know you live all by yourself in a lovely apartment. But I thought maybe at Christmas you'd go home to your family.

CARLA. No.

PATTY. Are they coming to see you?

CARLA. No.

PATTY. But where will you go for Christmas dinner?

CARLA. I'm dining at the Franklin Arms.

PATTY. Alone?

CARLA. Correct.

PATTY. Oh. (*They both resume their work as the telephone rings.*)

CHRISTMAS FOR CARLA

CARLA (*on the phone*). Baylor's Department Store. Miss Caldwell, personal shopper, speaking. . . . Yes, Mr. Davis, we have the perfume you returned. May I ask what was wrong with it? (*Her voice sharpens.*) Oh, indeed? You should have given me some idea of the young lady's personality. . . . What makes you think I'm annoyed? This shopping service is available to everyone, by phone or letter. . . . (*Sharply.*) No, it will not be necessary to write me a letter! . . . (*Raising her voice.*) I am not raising my voice! . . . Very well, if you prefer a gold charm bracelet, I'll find a nice one and send it to your office by messenger. . . . Pardon me, Mr. Davis, the term "personal shopper" doesn't mean I have time for personal conversation. Good-bye. (*Hangs up.*)

PATTY (*surprised*). You didn't talk very nice to Mr. Davis.

CARLA. Oh? (*Gets up, picking up the perfume box.*) It's the customer's privilege to change his mind.

PATTY. Almost as if you knew him and were sort of fighting with him.

CARLA (*going* R.). It so happens that I do know Jack Davis.

PATTY. A cranky old coot?

CARLA. No. (*As she is about to go out,* SALLY *comes in. She is in her late teens.*)

SALLY. Hi! This is my five-minute break and I dashed in here to get away from the noise in the toy department. (*Covers her ears and laughs.*)

PATTY. I know what you mean.

SALLY (*to* CARLA). You don't mind?

CARLA. If it's only for five minutes. (*Goes out* R.)

SALLY. Miss Frozen-Face is her usual sweet self, I see.

PATTY. I guess she just doesn't like Christmas.

SALLY (*sitting in easy chair*). Am I glad to sit down!

PATTY. I believe you.

SALLY. Did you ask her if you could get off early?

PATTY (*mimicking* CARLA). "You must learn not to make plans that conflict with your working hours."

SALLY. Doesn't she ever think of anything but her precious job?

PATTY. Maybe something's bothering her.

SALLY. Nothing bothers *her*. (*With enthusiasm.*) We're having Christmas dinner at my married sister's house.

PATTY. Oh, good.

SALLY. Eighteen relatives, imagine! And what a turkey!

PATTY. We're having turkey, too.

SALLY. I wonder what the elegant Miss Caldwell is having.

PATTY. She's dining alone at the Franklin Arms.

SALLY. Well, la-de-da!

PATTY. I've heard her say people get too sentimental over Christmas. (*Gets up.*) I feel mean talking about her like this. After all, she *is* fair. And very . . . well . . . efficient.

SALLY. Right. (*Glances at her watch and gets up.*) Duty calls.

(*There is a knock at* R. *and* AUNT NELLIE *comes in. She is a cheerful, plump woman in her sixties. She wears winter clothes and carries a shopping bag.*)

AUNT NELLIE. Excuse me, dear, are you the personal shopper?

SALLY. Goodness, no. I work in the toy department. (*Goes out* R.)

PATTY. I'm Miss Caldwell's secretary. Something I can do for you?

AUNT NELLIE. You can let me sit down and rest my feet, if you'll be so kind. Shopping really wears a person out.

PATTY. That chair's very comfortable.

AUNT NELLIE (*sitting down*). Thank you.

PATTY. You want to speak to Miss Caldwell?

AUNT NELLIE. All I want to do is rest my feet. This office seemed a likely refuge.

PATTY. Perfectly all right, I'm sure.

AUNT NELLIE. Don't let me keep you from your work.

PATTY. I like to be kept from my work. (*Laughs, but goes to her desk.*) But Miss Caldwell might give me a cold, cold look.

AUNT NELLIE. She'll forgive you, considering it's almost Christmas Eve.

PATTY (*sitting down*). You don't know our Miss Caldwell.

(CARLA *comes in* R. *with a bracelet box in her hand.*)

CARLA. If this bracelet doesn't suit him, he can just come over here and pick one out himself.

PATTY. This is Mrs. . . . (*Looks questioningly at* AUNT NELLIE.)

AUNT NELLIE. Mrs. Smith.

PATTY. She wants to rest her feet.

CARLA. Oh?

AUNT NELLIE. Such excitement and crowds, I really shouldn't have left any shopping to the last minute. But Christmas is more fun that way, don't you think?

CARLA. I've never thought about it. Patty, send this bracelet to Mr. Davis's office by messenger.

PATTY. Yes, Miss Caldwell. (*Peeks into box.*) He must think a lot of her!

CARLA. I bought the best. (*Sharply.*) And I hope he's satisfied this time!

(PATTY *goes out* R.)

AUNT NELLIE. You must find your work very interesting, buying things for people.

CARLA (*distantly, as she looks at papers*). Very.

AUNT NELLIE. When I was a girl, my young man would never ask someone else to do his shopping for him.

CARLA. Mr. Davis is a very busy lawyer. Such purchases are all in the day's work for me.

AUNT NELLIE. Nothing really personal about it at all?

CARLA. Of course not.

AUNT NELLIE. That's a pretty little tree you have.

CARLA. Patty brought it in.

AUNT NELLIE. The little ones are nice for an office, but there's nothing like a big one for home.

CARLA. I have no interest in Christmas trees of any size.

AUNT NELLIE. Now, now, you're much too young to talk like that.

CARLA. I prefer a Christmas without fuss and sentimentality.

AUNT NELLIE. Do you, now! I live in the country, myself, in a rambling farmhouse. (*After a pause.*) But I don't have much family left, now that my nephew has moved to the city.

CARLA. A modern apartment suits me very well.

AUNT NELLIE. But when your folks come? Or do you go home to them? (CARLA *lowers her head, busy.*) Sorry, you must think I'm an impertinent old woman.

CARLA. Aren't you?

AUNT NELLIE (*chuckling*). That's what my nephew often says.

CARLA. I didn't mean to be rude.

AUNT NELLIE. Nor I. It's just that I can't imagine anyone wanting to spend Christmas alone.

CARLA. Sometimes it's necessary to make a decision. I've made mine.

AUNT NELLIE. A young man?

CARLA. Perhaps.

(GINNY, *in her late teens, comes in* R. *She wears a coat and has a purse and the bracelet box.*)

GINNY. I came to see the personal shopper.

CARLA. What can I do for you?

GINNY. I'm Ginny Anderson, Mr. Davis's secretary.

CARLA. Yes?

GINNY. He says he hates to put you to so much trouble, but this isn't exactly what he wants. (*Puts the box on the desk.*)

CARLA (*annoyed*). Oh, it isn't! He gave me explicit instructions.

GINNY. I know, and he says he's very sorry.

CARLA. Does he think I have nothing else to do but buy gifts for him?

GINNY. Oh, it isn't for *him*.

CARLA (*giving* GINNY *a good look*). I understand now. *You* don't like it, I suppose?

GINNY (*puzzled*). Mr. Davis makes up his own mind.

CARLA. I just wish it would stay made up.

GINNY. He says he'll call you and explain. But since I was leaving for home, he asked me to stop by with this.

CARLA. Oh.

GINNY. I really didn't mind at all.

CARLA. I'm quite sure you didn't.

GINNY. He said, "Just tell Carla I'll call her." Does he know you?

CARLA. He does.

GINNY. Isn't he grand? I'm just crazy about him.

CARLA (*flatly*). How nice.

GINNY. Any girl would be, don't you think?

CARLA (*busy again*). I do not.

GINNY (*surprised*). Oh. Well, thank you for all your trouble.

CARLA. You're welcome. (*The telephone rings and she picks it up.* GINNY *goes out* R.) Oh, it's you again? Well, let me tell you, Jack Davis, I've had enough of this! (AUNT NELLIE *listens with interest.*) I don't care if it *is* my duty to speak politely to customers, I think you're doing it on purpose! . . . Why can't you find time to do your own shopping? . . . You want . . . what? (*Gasps.*) That's going too far. I absolutely refuse! (*Hangs up, very angry. Her cool aloofness is gone.*)

CHRISTMAS FOR CARLA

Aunt Nellie. Is he giving you trouble?

Carla. Do you know what he had the gall to ask? He wants me to meet him in the jewelry department and help him select an engagement ring!

Aunt Nellie. For his young lady?

Carla. His secretary, of course.

Aunt Nellie. A very pretty girl.

Carla (*rising, agitated*). But how can he ask me . . . *me* . . . to do it?

Aunt Nellie. I guess you know Mr. Davis pretty well.

Carla. Until two weeks ago I had the ridiculous idea that *I* was going to marry him.

Aunt Nellie. Oh, my! Some silly quarrel, I suppose.

Carla. A basic difference of opinion. I realized we could never be happy together.

Aunt Nellie. Oh?

Carla. I bought a new dress and planned that we'd have dinner together at the Franklin Arms. A modern, intelligent Christmas without drippy sentimentality.

Aunt Nellie. I see.

Carla. And then he came up with his medieval idea of going to his Aunt Nellie's farm for Christmas.

Aunt Nellie. You've never met his aunt?

Carla. No, and I don't intend to.

Aunt Nellie. Quite likely a fat old busybody.

Carla. Oh, I hardly think so. But I just don't want to get mixed up with relatives and farmhouses and Christmas fuss.

Aunt Nellie. I see.

CARLA. Jack says I'm too wrapped up in my job, and it's not half as important as I think it is.

AUNT NELLIE. Oh?

CARLA (*defensively*). I've worked hard to get where I am. I like new, modern things. I don't want to have anything to do with the old.

AUNT NELLIE. Maybe you don't know what he means by an old-fashioned Christmas, having lived in the city all your life.

CARLA. What makes you think I've always lived in the city? I know, all right.

AUNT NELLIE. Do you?

CARLA. I was born in an old-fashioned farmhouse like his aunt's. I had old-fashioned Christmases till I was seventeen.

AUNT NELLIE. Why did you stop having them at seventeen?

CARLA (*standing by the little Christmas tree*). That was when I went away to college. Right after my mother and father died.

AUNT NELLIE. Oh.

CARLA (*almost bitterly*). Yes, I know. Just your own family, because Christmas Eve isn't the time for outsiders. (*As she talks, her voice softens and takes on a lost quality.*) Your dad brings in the tree, so tall it reaches the ceiling and he has to cut off a little bit. . . .

AUNT NELLIE (*gently*). So tall.

CARLA. He holds the stepladder while you put the battered old star on top, and you know you ought to buy a new star, but you've always used that one, so you don't want a new one. . . .

AUNT NELLIE. A new one is never the same.

CARLA. All three of you decorate the tree to-

CHRISTMAS FOR CARLA 51

gether. You put on shining ornaments in a rainbow of colors. And you put on some old tarnished ones, too, because you've had them since you were a little girl and you love them. . . .

AUNT NELLIE. Yes.

CARLA. Best of all, you love the little silver trumpet that was on the very first Christmas tree that you remember. . . .

AUNT NELLIE. I know.

CARLA. And your mother brings in cocoa and sandwiches, and you eat by the fireplace. And you're so hungry, and the hot cocoa burns your tongue. . . .

AUNT NELLIE. Yes.

CARLA (*unaware of her now*). And your dad stands near the mistletoe and calls you over and kisses you on the cheek. And your mother laughs and hugs you. And you're all together, safe and secure, and they'll always be there to take care of you.

AUNT NELLIE. Yes.

CARLA. But you don't say this to them, because you don't know how to put it into words. So you go over to admire the tree. And you touch the little silver trumpet . . . just touch it . . . and it falls and breaks, and you cry. (*Suddenly she sits in* PATTY's *chair, burying her head in her arms.*) Silly to cry over a broken ornament after so many years.

AUNT NELLIE (*getting up*). You're not crying over the ornament. (*Goes to* CARLA.) You're crying for the lost years with your parents. Because you still miss them so much, you're afraid of Christmas.

CARLA (*looking up*). Afraid?

AUNT NELLIE. You've closed your heart because you won't risk being hurt.

CARLA. Maybe . . . that's true.

AUNT NELLIE (*a hand on* CARLA'S *shoulder*). We all lose something when we lose those early Christmases of our childhood. But if we keep our hearts open, other Christmases come along. And they're good when we share them with someone who loves us.

CARLA. Like Jack.

AUNT NELLIE. Yes, like Jack.

CARLA. When he asked me to spend Christmas with his Aunt Nellie, I was scornful and superior. (*Mocking herself.*) The sophisticated Miss Caldwell. What fun your work must be, Miss Caldwell!

AUNT NELLIE. They all say that?

CARLA. Fun? Buying for other people all the time. No one of my own to buy for. No one at all. (*Turns away.*)

AUNT NELLIE. So that's how it is.

CARLA. I've never talked this way to anyone.

(PATTY *and* SALLY *come in* R.)

PATTY. Sorry I took so long, Miss Caldwell. I'll get on those letters right away.

SALLY. We were both talking to Santa Claus on his coffee break.

CARLA (*softened now*). I hope he gives you both what you asked for. And, Patty, skip the letters. You may take the rest of the afternoon off.

PATTY (*pleased*). I may? Oh, thank you, Miss Caldwell!

SALLY. And a very merry Christmas! (*They go out* R.)

CARLA. It won't be exactly merry, but I have only myself to blame.

CHRISTMAS FOR CARLA 53

(*The telephone rings and* AUNT NELLIE *is nearer to it.*)

AUNT NELLIE. Shall I get it? (*On phone.*) Office of the personal shopper. . . . All right, Mr. Davis, I'll tell her. (*To* CARLA.) Jack Davis is downstairs at the ring counter waiting for you.

CARLA. He's daring me to come down, isn't he? (*Takes a deep breath.*) I'll go. I'll help him pick out a ring for another girl. (*With sarcasm.*) My wonderful, wonderful job!

AUNT NELLIE (*on phone*). She'll be right down. But she thinks you want the ring for your secretary. Shall I tell her? . . . I *thought* you'd finally recognize my voice! (*Hangs up.*)

CARLA (*startled*). What did you say?

AUNT NELLIE. He wants the ring for *you*.

CARLA. But . . . how do you know?

AUNT NELLIE. Jack sent me here because you wouldn't talk to him. I'm his Aunt Nellie.

CARLA. Oh. (*Happily.*) Oh!

AUNT NELLIE. So get going.

CARLA. I certainly will! (*Goes* R.)

AUNT NELLIE. Will I see the two of you at the farmhouse tonight for an old-fashioned Christmas?

CARLA. Try and keep us away! (*Goes out* R.)

(AUNT NELLIE *smiles after her. Then she picks up her shopping bag and goes slowly toward the door.*)

CURTAIN

THE MERRY-GO-ROUND GIFT
(For a Mixed Cast of Teen-Agers)

CHARACTERS

TESSA, *a busy teen.*
JIM, *her boy friend.*
KATHY
MARK } *their friends.*
JANIE

SCENE: Tessa's living room.
TIME: Christmas Eve.

(SCENE: *Tessa's living room. Curtain backdrops may be used. There are a sofa with coffee table, a couple of easy chairs, and a table with a telephone. Christmas decorations are in evidence: red candles, a bowl of evergreens, perhaps a small decorated tree on a table. An exit at* L. *leads outside, one at* R. *leads to other rooms.*)

(AT RISE OF CURTAIN: TESSA *is standing on a stepladder* U. C., *getting ready to hang a wreath with a large red bow on the wall behind the sofa. One or two small hooks are already in place. She holds it up to study the effect. The doorbell rings.*)

TESSA. Oh, dear! (*The bell rings again.*) Come in!

THE MERRY-GO-ROUND GIFT

(JIM *comes in* L.)

JIM. Hi, beautiful. Busy?

TESSA. You can say that again.

JIM. Busy. Me, too.

TESSA. I'm trying to decide the best place to hang this wreath.

JIM. Should look good right there.

TESSA. Maybe *you* . . . ?

JIM. Right now I have some shopping to do before the stores close.

TESSA (*sitting on top of the ladder*). Honestly, Jim, do you always do your shopping at the last minute?

JIM. Just one more gift to buy, for somebody very special.

TESSA. Oh?

JIM. Tessa, can you give me one little hint about what you'd like for Christmas?

TESSA. You know I like to be surprised.

JIM. As, for instance?

TESSA. Well . . . something sort of different and original.

JIM. That's not much help.

TESSA. I bought your gift a whole month ago.

JIM. Girls are better organized.

TESSA. I'm not well organized now. Mother's gone to a meeting and all the decorating is up to me.

JIM. Maybe I can stop back and help you.

TESSA. Don't spend too much on me, Jim. (*Stands up, trying the wreath again.*)

JIM. *Different* things usually cost a little more. (*Her back is to him. He takes out his wallet and quickly checks to see how much money he has. When she turns toward him again, he faces her, putting his wallet on an end table behind him.*)

TESSA. Not if you shop around a bit.

JIM. Not much time left to shop around. (*The doorbell rings.*) Expecting company?

(KATHY *comes in* L.)

KATHY. Only me. Hi, Tessa, Jim. I've come to borrow.

JIM. Excuse me if I run off. See you later! (*Goes out* L.)

KATHY. Nice fellow, Jim.

TESSA. He wants to buy a gift for me before the stores close.

KATHY. I wish him luck.

TESSA. Like the wreath up here? (*Holds it up.*)

KATHY. Looks good. But can you do it a little later?

(TESSA *gets down from the stepladder, putting the wreath on the sofa.*)

TESSA. What do you want to borrow?

KATHY. The punch bowl for my party tonight. You and Jim are coming, aren't you?

TESSA. Sure thing. I love Christmas parties.

KATHY. I thought I'd make little sandwiches, and I baked some cookies. . . . (*The doorbell rings.*) Who, now?

TESSA. I'll go see. (*Goes out* L.)

(KATHY *admires the bowl of evergreens, rearranging them a little.* TESSA *comes in with a long box wrapped in brown paper.*)

THE MERRY-GO-ROUND GIFT 57

Tessa. A package by special delivery. (*Looks at it.*) Oh, from my Great-Aunt Tessie in Fairfield City. M'mm. . . .

Kathy. Open it, open it! What do you suppose could be in a box that shape?

Tessa. I'm her namesake and she always sends me a Christmas present.

Kathy. Do you send her one?

Tessa. A box of fruit or candy from one of the mail order catalogs. (*Tugs at string.*)

Kathy. I hope she sends you something better than that.

Tessa. Aunt Tessie's gifts are always . . . unique. (*Gets a pair of scissors from the coffee table and cuts the string.*)

Kathy. Really nice?

Tessa. Well, she lives alone and she's forever taking adult school courses in things. Last year it was ceramics and she sent me . . . I suppose you might call it a pottery vase.

Kathy. Pretty? (*Looks around.*) I don't remember ever seeing it.

Tessa. Mother suggested that I put it in my room. That's where I put the piece of wire sculpture she sent me the year before.

Kathy. Sounds fascinating. (*Impatiently.*) Get that paper off the box!

(Tessa *lays the package on the coffee table and pulls off the brown paper, crumpling it. The box is decorated with a Christmas bow on the lid.*)

Tessa. All right so far.
Kathy. Hurry! I just know it's something great.

(TESSA *lifts the lid. She takes out a long painting in a simple frame, gives a little gasp, and holds it up. The painting may be done in poster paint. The kindest thing to call it is abstract art. It is a wild conglomeration of vivid colors and even at first glance it hurts the eyes.*)

TESSA (*weakly*). O-oh.

KATHY (*shocked*). Oh, my!

TESSA. This year she must have taken a course in painting.

KATHY. A . . . picture. Of what?

TESSA. I guess you'd call it abstract art.

KATHY. Yes, that's what it is, all right.

TESSA. Very . . . colorful.

KATHY (*brightly*). Really gorgeous colors.

TESSA. Different.

KATHY. You'll never find another one like it.

TESSA. All Aunt Tessie's gifts are . . . original.

KATHY. Oh, very.

TESSA. What do you think of it?

KATHY (*trying to be polite*). Very striking.

TESSA. You really like it?

KATHY. Do I! Where are you going to hang it?

TESSA. The colors aren't quite right for my room.

KATHY. What a pity. Such a beautiful painting!

TESSA. Kathy, I'll tell you what. Since you like it so much . . .

KATHY (*warily*). What I meant was . . .

TESSA. I'll give it to you! (*Puts the picture into* KATHY'S *hands.*)

KATHY (*dismayed*). Oh, no, I really couldn't accept it from you!

TESSA. We always exchange gifts, don't we? This is my gift to you.

THE MERRY-GO-ROUND GIFT

KATHY. But I . . . but, Tessa . . .

TESSA. Don't say another word. I'm glad you're crazy about it and I want you to have it.

KATHY. O-oh.

TESSA. Now, that punch bowl. It may take me a while to find where Mother put it. (*Goes out* R.)

(KATHY *props the picture up against the back of the sofa and backs away to look at it.*)

KATHY. Oh, why did I open my big mouth? (*Turns the picture upside down and looks again.*) Even worse! (*Stands it on end.*) A nightmare!

(*The doorbell rings.*)

TESSA (*calling from offstage*). Get it, will you?

KATHY (*calling*) Come in! (MARK *comes in* L. *carrying a box.*) Oh, hi, Mark.

MARK. Just delivering the fruitcake that Tessa's mother ordered. (*Puts it on table, then sees picture.*) Wow!

KATHY. It's an original. (*Turns it back on its long side.*) Look better now?

MARK (*politely*). Interesting, isn't it?

KATHY. Yes, very.

MARK. So bright.

KATHY. Do you like the colors?

MARK. Sensational!

KATHY. Honestly?

MARK. Would I say that if I didn't mean it?

KATHY. I'm so glad you like it. A wonderful present for your mother, don't you think?

MARK. Uh . . . sure. Only it's yours.

KATHY. The funniest thing, Mark. I've been doing so much Christmas shopping that I got my list sort of scrambled, and now I have one gift too many. This one.
MARK. Oh?
KATHY. Since you like it so much, it's yours. (*Puts the picture in his hands, goes* L., *then turns.*) I've decided to serve cocoa instead of punch. Be seeing you! (*Hurries out* L.)

(MARK *stands looking at the picture.*)

MARK. Mine. (*To picture.*) You . . . atrocity! Why did I try to be polite? Mother would have a fit. What am I going to *do* with you?

(*The doorbell rings.*)

TESSA (*calling*). See who it is! I'm still looking for the punch bowl.

(*The bell rings again and* JANIE *comes in.*)

JANIE. Tessa home?
MARK. She's busy with something.
JANIE. I just stopped by to talk, so I guess I'd better not stay.
MARK. I have to be going, myself. (*Looks at picture.*)
JANIE (*noticing it*). Whose . . . picture?
MARK. Mine. Like it?
JANIE (*politely*). Very . . . unusual.
MARK. My own opinion exactly.

THE MERRY-GO-ROUND GIFT

JANIE. Since Tessa's busy . . . (*Goes* L., *pauses.*) What I wanted to talk to her about, I'm redecorating my room, mostly neutral colors, and I thought she might have some ideas on how to brighten it up.

MARK (*going after her*). Don't go yet, Janie. Because you've come at just the right time.

JANIE. I have?

MARK. You say you like this picture?

JANIE. It's just . . . uh . . . darling.

MARK. A funny thing, I had so much shopping to do that I got my list kind of scrambled. And I find I have one gift too many. This.

JANIE. Really?

MARK. Since you're so crazy about it, you can have it. (*Puts it in her arms.*)

JANIE (*stunned*). Me? Oh, no!

MARK. Don't try to thank me, just enjoy it.

JANIE (*weakly*). This?

MARK. The perfect thing to brighten up your room!

JANIE. It would do that, all right.

MARK. Glad it makes you happy. 'Bye, now! (*Hurries out* L.)

JANIE. Happy? (*Comes back* C., *looking at picture.*) I'd get the screaming meemies! This is the last time I'll be polite about something I don't like. (*Sees the box with the decorated lid.*) Back you go in your box. (*Puts it in.*) Let me get the lid on fast! (*Puts on the lid.*)

(*The doorbell rings rapidly several times and* JIM *comes in.*)

JIM. Hi, Janie. (*Unhappily.*) I've had the worst luck! Got to the best store in town just before it closed, reached for my wallet . . . gone!

JANIE. Oh, Jim, what a shame!

JIM. I had it when I was here, checking my money. . . . I wonder . . . (*Looks around, sees wallet on end table.*) Here it is! (*Grabs it.*)

JANIE. Now you feel better.

JIM. I was sure I'd lost it.

JANIE. You can go back and buy whatever it is you wanted.

JIM (*sighing*). Oh, no, I can't. (*Looks at his watch.*) Too late, store's closed now. (*Sits down, dejected.*)

JANIE. Was it an important gift?

JIM. For Tessa.

JANIE. Oh, I'm so sorry.

JIM. She said she wanted something different, original. I still don't know what I should have bought her.

JANIE (*perking up*). Different?

JIM. You know how Tessa is, she likes to be surprised.

JANIE. Jim, things have the strangest way of happening.

JIM. Don't they, though? Here I am with no gift for her.

JANIE. I want you to have a look at something and give me your honest opinion.

JIM. Sure, what?

JANIE. This picture. (*Takes it out of the box.*) Well?

JIM (*trying to be enthusiastic*). Well!

JANIE. It's abstract art.

THE MERRY-GO-ROUND GIFT 63

Jim. So that's what they call it.
Janie. Did you ever see such color?
Jim. Can't say I ever did.
Janie. And, Jim, it's original!
Jim. I believe you.
Janie. The funniest thing, I had so many gifts to buy that I got my Christmas list sort of scrambled and now I have one extra gift. This one.
Jim. Extra?
Janie. And since you need a gift for Tessa, and you like this one so much . . .
Jim. Now, wait a minute, Janie . . . you like it yourself, and it wouldn't be fair . . .
Janie. I won't take no for an answer. (*Puts the picture in* Jim's *arms.*) The perfect gift for Tessa! (*Goes* L.) See you! (*Goes out* L.)
Jim. *This* is a perfect gift? (*Half to himself.*) I know she likes art work, but . . . abstract, huh? Me, I don't know a thing about it. (*Holds up picture, looking at it.*) Art? Maybe I'm just too ignorant to know. (*Sighs as he puts the picture back in its box.*) Maybe Tessa *does* like this kind of stuff.

(Tessa *comes in* R. *with a large box.*)

Tessa. I finally found the punch bowl. Where's Kathy?
Jim. Not here when I came. Just Janie, and she left.
Tessa (*putting down the box*). I guess she couldn't have wanted this punch bowl very much. (*Notices box in* Jim's *hands.*) What's that?
Jim. You know I dashed down to buy your Christmas gift.

TESSA. The stores weren't closed?

JIM. They are now, but I have something I do hope you'll like.

TESSA. That's it?

JIM. Merry Christmas, Tessa. (*Puts the box in her hands.*)

TESSA. Thank you, Jim. (*Looks at box.*) This must be my year for getting boxes that look alike.

JIM. You'll never get another gift like this one. Open it.

TESSA. I'd better wait 'til Christmas day.

JIM. Please open it. I want to make sure you really like it.

TESSA. I'm sure I'll like anything you give me.

JIM. I'd feel better if you opened it now.

TESSA. Silly! You act worried.

JIM. I guess I am.

TESSA. But of course I'll like it! (*Sets box on coffee table and takes off the lid.*) Oh! (*Lifts up picture and stands looking at it.*)

JIM. It's . . . different, isn't it?

TESSA. Quite different.

JIM. Some day I'll tell you how I happened to get it. I did so want to give you something you'd like.

TESSA. That's sweet of you.

JIM. You don't think the colors are too bright?

TESSA (*bravely*). Jim, I adore it!

JIM (*pleased*). I'm glad. What I mean is, different people like different things.

TESSA. They certainly do.

JIM. Want me to hang it up for you now, instead of that wreath?

TESSA (*gulping*). Here?

JIM. That wall's a perfect spot. (*Takes the pic-*

ture from TESSA *and starts up the stepladder.*) Tell me when I have it straight.

TESSA (*half to herself*). Oh, why did Aunt Tessie . . . every year, this same kind of problem. . . .

JIM. No problem at all to hang it.

TESSA. The best thing she had to give, I guess. Maybe the only thing.

JIM. Where's the picture hook? Oh, here. (*Puts picture on it.*)

TESSA. Reaching out to me because I'm her namesake. . . . Poor Aunt Tessie, she must feel so alone at Christmas. . . .

JIM. What are you talking about?

TESSA. We're always so busy with our own affairs at Christmas that we haven't given her a thought. . . .

JIM. Is it straight now? (*Adjusts the picture.*)

TESSA. Jim, Fairfield City isn't so very far. Would you mind missing the Christmas party tonight?

JIM. Not if you say so.

TESSA. We could drive there and pick up my old Aunt Tessie, bring her here to spend Christmas with us.

JIM. Sure. What made you think of her, all of a sudden?

TESSA. I'll tell you after a while. Right now, I have a phone call to make. (*Looks in a little phone book.*) Mother has the number here. . . . (*Finds the number and speaks into the telephone, giving it.*) Hello . . . Tessa calling. Aunt Tessie, would you like to spend Christmas with us? . . . We can be there for you in a couple of hours. . . .

JIM (*down from ladder, looking up at picture*). Sure you like it?

TESSA (*covering the receiver*). There's something about it that's almost beautiful! (*Into phone.*) Then start packing your bag! 'Bye, now. (*Hangs up.*)

JIM (*looking up at picture*). Beautiful? (TESSA *stands beside him and nods her head.*)

CURTAIN

CHRISTMAS TREES FOR SALE

CHARACTERS

TOM MASON, *a middle-aged business man.*
MARIE MASON, *his wife.*
PAULA MASON, *their twenty-year-old daughter.*
THE CHRISTMAS TREE VENDOR, *an old man.*
BILL FARNUM, *a young man.*

    SCENE: The Mason living room.
    TIME: Christmas Eve.

(SCENE: *The room is one of those into which one steps directly upon opening the front door, and it is the front door that we are facing—a dignified, paneled door, painted white. To* L. *and* R. *are windows, attractively draped and each bearing an artificial Christmas wreath. Between door and windows are small tables bearing matched vases with sprays of Christmas greens—artificial but not obviously so. In* L. *wall is a door and in* R. *wall, extreme rear, a stairway leads to the second floor. At* R. *front is a comfortable davenport with end tables beside it. On them are a low bowl of Christmas greens—also artificial—an ash tray and a lamp. At* L. *front is a substantial table with a handsome table cover* [*that falls over the edge as much as the prevailing fashion allows*] *and a book or two. Below table is straight chair and, to* R. *of it, an easy chair. At* L. *wall, rear, is a small table with a mirror above it.*)

(*The rising curtain discovers* TOM MASON *seated on the davenport, smoking his pipe and enjoying his evening paper. He is middle-aged. His hair is growing thin and his waistline proportionately thick. He wears a smoking jacket, comfortable house slippers, and bone-rimmed spectacles. He turns a page, scans its contents, then, cocking an attentive ear toward the stairs, quickly removes his pipe and, with an affectionate glance at it, lays it with a sigh in the ash tray and is busy with his paper again as* MARIE MASON, *his wife, comes down the stairs. She is a good-looking woman in her late forties. Her expression is pleasant but somewhat strained. She wears a simple afternoon dress. She is carrying a box, about the size of a large suit box, and on top of it something about two feet long, wrapped in tissue paper. She crosses toward the table, but stops at* C. *stage to sniff the air. Her eyes turn accusingly toward her husband.*)

MARIE. Tom, you've been smoking that pipe again.

TOM (*deep in his paper*). M-h-m.

MARIE. I've asked you so often not to smoke in here.

TOM. M-h-m.

MARIE. Yes, that's all you ever say: M-h-m! I should think when you want to smoke you could go up to your den instead of filling the living room with tobacco smell.

TOM (*lowering his paper and looking over his glasses*). It's a perfectly good, natural, homey smell. (*He sees the packages.*) Hello—what you got there?

CHRISTMAS TREES FOR SALE 69

MARIE (*passing to* L. *of table and setting them on chair*). I never can understand why things get so dusty up in the attic. I keep everything covered, but you'd never know it.

TOM (*chuckling*). Oh, wouldn't I! Every time I go up there, I get so tangled up in sheets I scare myself. I begin to think maybe I'm a ghost. (MARIE *is unwrapping the tissue paper package.*) What you got there?

MARIE (*rather defensively*). If you must know, it's a Christmas tree. (*She brings forth and holds at arm's length appraisingly a decidedly scrawny-looking artificial tree, with its collapsible branches folded tight so that it looks rather like a second-hand umbrella.*)

TOM (*laying aside his paper, removing glasses, and returning them to a case in his pocket*). Good heavens! Don't tell me you call that a tree! Where in the world'd you get it?

MARIE. Why, you remember. I won it as a prize at the Church Fair. It's been up in the attic ever since. I'd completely forgotten it.

TOM. Too bad you didn't keep right on forgetting it.

MARIE (*shaking the thing and bending its branches down*). After all, it isn't Christmas without some kind of tree.

TOM. Well, why didn't you say so? I'd have bought a real one!

MARIE. I didn't realize I was going to mind so much.—But there aren't any good ones left by this time and those that are left they charge outrageous prices for. I brought the ornaments down— (*nods toward the box*) though this won't take anywhere near all of them.

TOM (*rising to walk over to the table and stand, hands in pockets, watching his wife while she sets the tree on its wobbly standard on the table, pushing and pulling it this way and that to give it some semblance of life*). They had some fine ones down at Griggs'— but I s'pose they'd be gone by now.

MARIE. Of course they would. (*She speaks with a forced conviction.*) And—a real one's a lot of bother, anyhow. Sheds needles all over the place.

TOM. Not if you get a fir tree.

MARIE. Well, it seems to me I'm still picking them off the floor at Eastertime.

TOM (*rather wistfully*). Yeh, I s'pose so. Still— it's the first year we haven't had a tree.

MARIE (*defensively again*). But you felt the same way I did about it. I thought we'd decided this year we'd better not have a tree.

TOM. I know, but—wait a minute. Wouldn't that thing look better this way? (*He turns and pulls it a bit, then stands back to regard his efforts quizzically.*) Of all the bedraggled, forlorn-looking objects—

MARIE. Tom, you're so discouraging! When I'm trying to make the place look a little like Christmas—

TOM (*laughing shortly and beginning to prowl restlessly around the room*). Christmas my eye! It's not my idea of Christmas. Artificial tree—artificial wreaths—artificial greens— (*He makes sweeping gestures toward table, windows, and vases.*) Oh, I know they look real enough at a distance, but they're still artificial. (*He continues his prowling.*) By golly! All we need now is to turn on the T.V. and get a few canned Christmas carols and everything'll be just dandy. (*His walk ends beside the ash tray. He picks up his pipe and examines it fondly.*) Won't it? (*At the beginning of his tirade* MARIE *has stood staring before her, nervously clasping and unclasping her hands, but by the time he finishes she has turned away and is crying quietly into her handkerchief. At the continued silence he looks up. Quickly he lays down the pipe and with a few long strides is beside her, an arm around her shoulders.*) Marie! What's wrong? What's the matter with me!—Listen, dear, I didn't mean it. Everything looks just great. I guess my nerves are just a bit on edge—that's all. Cheer up, honey. It's all right.

MARIE (*wiping her eyes and leaning her head wearily against his shoulder*). You might remember that I may not be feeling any better than you do.

TOM. I know! I know! (*He hesitates.*) It's—Paula, isn't it?

MARIE. Of course it's Paula. (*She turns impetuously and clings to his arm.*) Tom, I'm worried to death about her. She isn't herself lately.

TOM (*his face suddenly old and haggard*) I know.—(*He leads her to the davenport, where he sits more or less comfortably, and she perches tensely on the edge.*) I thought she seemed a little more cheerful at dinner tonight.

MARIE. Cheerful, yes—that awful forced cheerfulness because she knew we were watching and worrying about her. But when you catch her off guard, she's sitting there staring into space.

TOM. Sitting quiet is the last thing in the world Paula ever did.

MARIE. Of course it is—and once or twice when I've come on her suddenly, I know she's been crying.

TOM. Why not ask her what the trouble is? After all, you're her mother.

MARIE. I've tried, but she just turns it off lightly and braces up for a while.

TOM. It's agony to be a parent and have to watch a cute little kid like that getting hurt and not be able to step in and fix things for her.

MARIE. I know, but (*she makes a helpless gesture*) what can we do unless we know what's bothering her. And apparently she doesn't intend to tell.

TOM. Where is she now?

MARIE. Up in her room, getting ready to go out dancing again.

TOM. That's the—let's see—second—third—fourth time this week, isn't it?

MARIE. Yes. And, Tom—this is Christmas Eve.

TOM. Yeh—I was thinking of that. First Christmas Eve she's ever been away from us. You remember how—

MARIE (*jumping up and walking to the table*). Don't! Don't—not just now. I'm trying not to remember.

TOM. Where's she going tonight?

MARIE. I don't know.

TOM (*lowering his voice*). Careful—I hear her coming. (*He picks up his paper.*)

MARIE (*busies herself with the tree again*). There! I think that looks as natural as it ever will. Now when I get a few ornaments on it— (*In the course of the following scene she takes three or four ornaments from the box and puts them on the tree.* PAULA *descends the stairs.*) Oh, there you are,

CHRISTMAS TREES FOR SALE

Paula. I was wondering whether you wanted any help with your dress.

(PAULA *is a pretty girl of twenty, but just now much too restless to appear at her best. She wears a beautiful evening gown and carries a bright-colored evening coat over her arm and in one hand an evening bag and a pair of white gloves.*)

PAULA. Oh, thanks. I got along all right. (*She lays bag, coat, and gloves on davenport and crosses* L. *to stand before mirror and give a few ineffectual and unnecessary pats to her hair.*)

TOM. Seems to me some folks look pretty special tonight.

PAULA (*dully*). Thanks, Dad. I feel—great.

TOM. Er—who's the young gallant this time?

PAULA. Jerry Whiting.

MARIE. Oh, Paula! Not Marsden Whiting's son?

PAULA. Why not?

MARIE. Well, he's not—just your kind, is he?

(PAULA *comes to* C. *stage and, picking up her gloves, starts pulling one on.*)

PAULA. Oh, I don't know. He's got looks, lots of cash, a new car, a fast line. . . . What more can a girl ask?

MARIE. But, Paula, I—

TOM (*interrupting*). Sounds like all the ingredients for a good time—of a sort. (*Casually.*) Where's the dance?

PAULA. Nowhere in particular. We'll probably hit all the high spots.

MARIE. Paula— (*She hesitates, then starts again.*) Dear, wouldn't you rather stay home—just tonight?

PAULA. And sit under the sheltering branches of (*she laughs scornfully*) our Christmas tree?

TOM. We could play games—the way we used to on Christmas Eve.

(PAULA, *having inched her way into one glove, wanders around to the back of the davenport and starts on the other one.*)

PAULA (*in dull, measured tones*). I'm tired of playing games. I don't have very good luck at them.

MARIE. Why, dear, you always used to win when we—

PAULA (*interrupting*). Dad, your hair's getting thin on top.

TOM (*leaning his head back to look up at her*). That's where a little girl I used to know always kissed me. Maybe it'll grow in again now.

PAULA (*in a choked voice*). Dad, I— (*She bends quickly and kisses the top of his head, then continues more lightly.*) There! There's another hair gone—and all your fault, too. (*An auto sounds off stage.*) Oh, that's Jerry now—and does that boy hate to be kept waiting. (*She throws the coat around her, seizes the bag, crosses quickly to* MARIE, *and kisses her lightly. The horn blows an insistent summons.*) 'Bye, Mom.

MARIE. You'll be careful, dear, won't you?

PAULA. Oh, sure. (*She crosses to door, back.*) 'Bye, Dad. Be seeing you. (*She opens the door.*)

TOM. Not too late, honey.

CHRISTMAS TREES FOR SALE 75

PAULA (*with a metallic laugh*). Late? Don't worry. It'll be very early when Little Paula gets home. (*The door closes.* TOM *rises, strides to the window,* L., *and stands looking out. Almost at once he turns back.*)

TOM. Insolent young puppy! Lolling there honking his horn at her. No more manners than he has morals. And they're off like a streak of greased lightning.

MARIE. Tom, why *didn't* you forbid her to go?

TOM. And have her go, anyhow? The way she's feeling, she'd have done it, sure as shooting. No, she's far enough away from us now. We mustn't drive her any further off.

(MARIE *has sunk into chair* R. *of table and sits with head leaning back, eyes closed, and arms resting along the arms of the chair.* TOM *stands behind her.*)

MARIE (*like one who is finally giving way to what she has been refusing*). Oh, I do remember. I do remember!

TOM. Remember what, dear?

MARIE. All those other Christmases.

TOM. We've had a lot of happy ones—the three of us.

MARIE. Always the three of us and always the Christmas tree the center of things.

TOM. By golly, we've had some fine trees—high as the ceiling and full of the smell of pine woods. Yup, we've been through some lean years but always there's been the Christmas tree.

MARIE. And Paula always helped us trim it.

Tom. Funny little tyke! Trotting around after us, always getting underfoot and putting all the ornaments in the wrong places. I never saw a kid enjoy a tree more than she did.

Marie. And the games we played afterwards— with Paula bossing us within an inch of our lives.

Tom. And the coffee and pie we always had on leave for Santa Claus. It was good pie, too—homemade—I can taste it yet. (*He returns to davenport.*)

Marie. Do you remember the year we sneaked into her room just before we went to bed and tied a branch of evergreen to the bedpost? And just as we were tiptoeing out, she woke up and called, "Oh, he's come. Santa's come. I smell him."

Tom (*with a sigh*). Well, I s'pose all kids outgrow that sort of thing. We're probably trying to keep her a little girl. And it can't be done.

Marie. There's something more to it than that. Paula's unhappy. We've always known before what to do about it. But, Tom, I'm more and more convinced that this time we've failed her.

Tom. Failed her? But how—

Marie. If only we'd realized it sooner! Why, this year we should have had a grander Christmas than ever for her instead of—this. (*She waves a disdainful hand at the tree and the decorations.*) This year of all years it should have been—real.

Tom. But we talked it over, you know—

Marie. We thought we'd better go light on the sentiment because she seemed so close to tears. But we were wrong. We should have borne down hard on it—made her feel all the old familiar supports around her. She's always loved Christmas, and now

CHRISTMAS TREES FOR SALE

—just when she needs it—we've taken it away from her.

Tom. She didn't seem interested. She said she didn't care for a tree.

Marie. She's in no condition to know what she wants. But we should have known. Christmas—the real kind of Christmas—would have softened her, made her turn to us. Instead of that, we've driven her away from us—and on Christmas Eve.

Tom (*up and prowling around again*). Well, it's too late to think about that now. Besides, as you said a few minutes ago, it *is* a nuisance—messes up your room—and it's about time you began to think about yourself.

Marie (*jumping up*). What does it matter if we wade in pine needles an inch deep from now 'til June? Tom, we've got to have a tree!

Tom. Yes, but where—

Marie. It doesn't have to be a big one. She's got over being impressed by size. Not a big one, but a perfect one. A Christmas tree means something important to her—something we've built into her through all the years—and there's got to be one here for her when she gets home. It will really be the test of whether all those other Christmases have done what we wanted them to do for her. (*Hastily she removes the few ornaments that are already on the tree, folds up the tree, and lays it under the table in the cover of the box.*)

Tom (*watching operations doubtfully*). Well, I s'pose I could run down to Griggs' and see what he— (*He is interrupted by a knock at the door—not loud, but clear and measured.*) What's that?

Marie. Sounds like someone knocking.

Tom. No one knocks at the door when there's a bell to ring. (*The knock is repeated.* Tom *steps to the window.*) Some beggar, probably.

Marie. Well, Tom, you could open the door and find out.

(Tom *steps to the door and opens it wide, revealing on the threshold an old man, alert and straight, with finely chiseled features. He wears no hat, and his mass of white hair flows back from a noble forehead. A long black cloak completely envelops him. Standing before him on a firm stand is a small Christmas tree—small but beautifully shaped—a perfect tree. His voice is clear and bell-like.*)

Vendor. Christmas trees for sale! Will you buy?

Tom. By golly, you're the very man we want. I was just this minute going out to see if I could get a tree. C'm in.

Vendor (*stepping in*). Thank you. (*With respectful dignity he bows to* Marie.) Good evening, madam.

Marie. How do you do. (*She goes toward him.*) Oh, it's a lovely tree, Tom—exactly what we want.

Vendor. It's your tree—not big, but perfect.

Tom. Just what you said a minute ago, Marie.

Vendor. A tree full of the smell of pine woods—with fragments of bird song tangled in its branches—and perhaps a star or two.

Tom (*walking around it*). Paula ought to like that. Standard go with it?

Vendor. Its roots strike deep within your hearts. It will stand firm and true.

CHRISTMAS TREES FOR SALE

MARIE. It's as beautiful a tree as I've ever seen.

VENDOR. More beautiful, for it has cost you more.

TOM. Oh, we know we waited pretty late. How much?

VENDOR. More than any tree you've ever had. Before you always paid for your tree with loving thoughts and sacrificial labor—that is the price of every Christmas tree—but this one you buy with yearning and prayer. (*With a tender smile he turns toward* MARIE.) Is that not so?

MARIE (*her eyes on his*). How could you have known? Yes—with yearning for her confidence, with prayers for her safety and her happiness.

TOM (*puzzled by the conversation*). But how much? A dollar? A dollar and a half?

VENDOR (*stepping forward and setting the tree in the center of the table*). Nothing. You have paid the price and the tree is yours.

TOM. But—we can't do that, you know. You'll have to—

(MARIE, *passing to* L. *of table, now stands below it, looking with shining eyes first at the tree, then at the* VENDOR.)

MARIE. Excuse me, but—who are you? You look so familiar.

VENDOR. You have known me for many years. I am a vendor of Christmas trees. On every street corner and at every door I offer my wares at this Christmas season, but there are few who have the price—the price of tender memories, high courage, and shining hope. (*He turns toward the door and has his hand on the latch as* TOM *speaks.*)

Tom. Wait a minute. Can't we— Say! How about a cup of coffee and a piece of pie? (*He chuckles.*) We always used to leave that out for Santa Claus, and you're a sort of Santa Claus, you know—bringing a tree just when we needed it.

Vendor. You have already fed me with nectar and ambrosia.

Tom (*completely at a loss*). Well, in that case— Then there isn't anything we can do in return for—

Vendor. One gift you will give me.

Marie. Oh, I'm so glad! What is it?

Vendor. I have a helper—a young man; the young are always my helpers. You will let him help you decorate your tree, for he too has bought a share in it with yearning and prayer.

Marie. Why, of course. We'll be glad to have him.

Tom. Sure. Send him in.

(*The* Vendor *opens the door and beckons outside. An ordinary, good-looking young man appears, dressed in a dark suit and wearing a soft felt hat, which he removes as he steps in. His name is* Bill.)

Vendor. You will stay here to yield your share to the beauty of this tree.

Bill. Thank you, sir.

(*The* Vendor, *standing in the open door, raises his hand in a gesture of benediction.*)

Vendor. My blessing on all who come this night beneath this roof! May their hearts find peace and joy within the sheltering branches of the Christmas tree. May their memories and their hopes, their ambitions and their loves draw from it strength to greet another year.

> (*The door closes behind him. The three stand silent a second, then turn toward one another with a faint, self-conscious laugh.*)

MARIE. Well! I—I feel as if I were in church.

TOM. Queer old duffer! You been working for him long?

BILL. I never saw him before 'til tonight.

MARIE. But he said you were his helper.

TOM. We might as well get at this job and not take too much of your time. Sure you want to help?

BILL. Of course—if you'll let me.

MARIE (*indicating the box*). Here are the ornaments. It won't take any time with the three of us working on it. (*As they talk, the tree is quickly trimmed.*)

TOM. You say you never saw that old fellow 'til tonight?

BILL. No. It seems queer as I look back on it. I was walking along and suddenly there he was, standing on the corner, head flung back and voice clear as a bell, calling, "Christmas trees for sale." There were people going by, paying no attention—

TOM. Folks are apt to be pretty busy on Christmas Eve.

BILL. Then he turned, looked straight at me, and said, "Come with me."

MARIE. And then—

BILL (*laughing*). Well, I came, that's all. Somehow I had to.

MARIE. He has a compelling eye, almost as if he were—a king.

TOM. I'll bet we're keeping you from something you ought to be doing.

BILL. But you're not. I was just doing what I've been doing every evening lately.

TOM. What's that?

MARIE. Why, Tom!

TOM (*chuckling*). Well, I s'pose that is a bit personal.

BILL. I don't mind, only—it'll sound rather queer to you. I've been walking up one street and down another, looking in all the lighted windows where the shades are up.

TOM. Well! Not a second-story man, are you?

BILL (*throwing back his head and laughing—an honest young laugh*). I don't wonder you think so. It sounds suspicious. But my talents don't lie in that direction. I might say quite the opposite. Fact is— I'm a law student. Graduate in another year.

MARIE. Oh, how nice! We always said if we'd had a son we'd have liked him to be a lawyer.

TOM. Well, maybe you do a Peeping Tom business as a side line.

BILL. Wrong again! No, I'm just looking— (*his face grows serious*) looking for something I—lost.

MARIE (*puzzled*). Something you lost?

BILL. Well—someone.

TOM. Here's good luck to you in finding—him? (*There is the slightest interrogation in the last word.*)

BILL (*briefly*). Her.

TOM. Oh.

BILL. You trimming the tree for yourselves?

CHRISTMAS TREES FOR SALE

MARIE. No, for our little girl.

TOM. Only child—always had a tree.

BILL. Lucky child! I never had one—a tree, I mean.

(*By now the tree is shining with ornaments and by a common impulse they step back to admire it.*)

TOM. Not bad, eh?

MARIE. It's lovely.

BILL. I shan't ever forget this tree. Somehow I feel as if it were—partly mine.

MARIE. You certainly ought to have a share in it. You've helped make it lovely.

TOM (*looking into the box*). No more ornaments?

MARIE. No, we've used everything that— Tom!

TOM. What's the matter?

MARIE. Where's the star?

TOM. The star?

MARIE. Of course. The star that always goes on top.

TOM (*rummaging in the box*). Must be here somewhere.

BILL. I don't think there's anything more there. I felt around pretty thoroughly when I took out the last ball.

MARIE. But we've got to have a star, Tom. It wouldn't be her tree without a star on top!

TOM (*giving up the search and putting the box under the table*). It must have got mislaid when we put the things away last year. It certainly isn't here.

MARIE. Oh, dear! And she'll look for the star first of all.

BILL (*with a deep bow*). Madam, the little girl shall have her star. I go to capture one. (*He crosses to davenport and picks up his hat.*)

MARIE. Oh, no, you mustn't. Really you mustn't.

TOM. Of course not. 'Tisn't worth your going after it.

BILL. I had orders to help trim that tree, and it isn't trimmed until we have a star. Why, if I fell down on the job, those piercing eyes would haunt me. (*He starts for door, rear.*) I'll be back in a jiffy!

TOM. Well, look—if you're bound to go, the nearest place is Griggs'—two blocks over—and you'll save time if you go out the side door.

BILL. Fine!

TOM (*leading the way off,* L.). I'll leave the latch off for you— (*They exit.* MARIE *arranges an ornament to her greater satisfaction, then sits on the davenport to admire the tree.* TOM *returns, chuckling.*) Say, that's a fine young fellow. No foolishness about him.

MARIE. Isn't he nice! I took to him the minute he came in. And I feel so much easier with the tree all up. But it's a shame for him to— (*She stops and listens attentively.*) Listen!

TOM. I don't hear anything.

MARIE. A key in the lock. It can't be Paula so soon.

TOM. You must be imagining—

(*But the door opens and closes again quickly to admit* PAULA. *She stands, back to the door, arms spread against it, and head flung back.*)

MARIE. Paula! We didn't—

CHRISTMAS TREES FOR SALE

PAULA (*with a bitter laugh*). They say a bad penny always— (*She stops, seeing the tree, takes a few steps forward and speaks almost in a whisper.*) Oh! You did get one. I— (*All her bright, hard shell shattered, she buries her face in her hands and sobs.*) Oh, I can't stand it! I can't stand it!

MARIE (*rising and going to her*). Oh, my dear—

TOM (*coming from other direction*). Paula, honey, what is it?

(PAULA *shakes her head, reaches for her dainty handkerchief, and continues weeping into it. Between them they lead her to the davenport,* TOM *removing her coat and laying it on end of davenport. She continues to sob.* MARIE *and* TOM *look at each other.* TOM *shakes his head hopelessly.* MARIE *sits beside* PAULA *and puts a comforting hand on her knee.* TOM *paces the room. The sobs lessen.*)

PAULA (*shakily*). Dad—

TOM (*turning to her quickly*). Right here, honey.

PAULA. Lend me a hankie, will you? These silly little things—

TOM (*fishing in a pocket*). Sure. Got an extra one just for the occasion. (*He extracts from his pocket a large handkerchief, neatly folded, shakes it out, and hands it to her.*) There you are. (*He sits in the easy chair.*)

PAULA. Thanks. (*The handkerchief is vigorously applied, there are a few more sniffs, then she sits up with decision, pushes her hair back, and grins sheepishly.*) Well, I guess that episode's over. And what a mess I must look!

Tom. You look mighty good to us.

Marie. Darling, we're so glad you came home.

Paula. I'm home for the first time in three weeks. And do you know what did it? That precious little Christmas tree. I didn't know how much I'd missed it.

Tom. Nice tree, isn't it?

Paula. I think it's the loveliest tree we've ever had.

Marie. But, dear, you didn't see the tree till you got here. Why did you come home? Weren't you having a good time?

Paula (*scornfully*). Good time! Can any decent girl have a good time with Jerry Whiting?

Marie (*with satisfaction*). I knew he wasn't your sort.

Tom. But you went out with him.

Paula. Only to get away from myself. He must be still wondering what got into me to leave him flat. But the strangest thing happened.

Marie. What was it?

Paula. We were driving along slowly—

Tom. Slowly! With that speed demon?

Paula. Oh, it was in traffic downtown. Anyhow, all at once I saw an old man standing on a street corner. He had flowing white hair and a long black cloak and oh! such a beautiful face.

Marie (*looking at* Tom). How strange!

(Tom *nods*.)

Paula. He was calling "Christmas trees for sale," and no one was paying any attention to him. Then, just as we passed, he turned and looked right at me and— (*She stops uncertainly.*)

MARIE (*gently*). Yes, dear?

PAULA. I don't quite know how to say it, but in his eyes I saw all the Christmas trees we've ever had and all the happiness they represented and—well, I just had to come home.

TOM (*hesitantly*). You wouldn't want to tell us what's been troubling you lately, would you?

MARIE. Don't urge her, dear.

TOM. I'm not urging her. I only thought—

(PAULA *rises and, as she talks, goes behind* TOM's *chair to* L. *of table, fondles an ornament or two, and finally sits in chair below table.*)

PAULA. Of course I'll tell you. I've wanted to, right along. I know what a hateful little beast I've been but I was so miserable—

MARIE. We understand, dear.

PAULA. Well, about three weeks ago our crowd went dancing at the Green Star. All of a sudden there was a young man standing beside me. Then just as suddenly we were dancing.

MARIE. Oh, Paula, not someone you didn't know!

PAULA. I knew him better than people I've known all my life. And he felt the same way about me.

TOM. What makes you think he did?

PAULA (*simply*). He said so. His name was Bill. Just to tease him I wouldn't tell him mine, but he said he'd find me if he had to look all over the world. I told him I always vanished suddenly into thin air. So after a while I just slipped out and came home.

MARIE. Well, really, Paula, if you wanted—

PAULA. Oh, I know. I came to my senses when I

got into the dressing room and decided I'd better help him a bit on the finding. I took my calling card and wrote my address on it. One of the page boys was standing at the door, so I gave it to him and said, "Give this to that young man across the room —the one leaning against the pillar. His name is Bill."

TOM. Well, then, if he'd wanted to find you—

PAULA. Next morning Bill Reynolds called up to know what the joke was.

MARIE. Oh, my dear! He'd given it to the wrong boy?

PAULA (*shrugging*). Sure. That's the way things happen. And I've gone back to the Green Star every time I could induce anyone to take me, but he's never been there.

TOM. And that's caused all the electrical disturbance in the air? We've been imagining all sorts of dreadful things.

PAULA. Oh, don't laugh. It *is* dreadful. It sounds silly to you, but—well, he's Bill and—he's the only one.

MARIE. But, child—after just one meeting—

PAULA. I've been feeling tragic and resentful, but now— If it's meant to be, he'll find me somehow and if not—well, I can't make myself and everyone else miserable the rest of my life.—Oh, how good that Christmas tree smells! I had no idea you were going to get one. And I wasn't even here to help you trim it.

(*A faint knocking is heard off,* L.)

MARIE. What's that, Tom?

Tom. I bet I put the latch on instead of off. (*He hurries out,* L.)

Paula (*rising*). It's not company, is it?

Marie. He's the nicest young man. He's been helping us trim the tree.

Paula (*completely uninterested*). Oh, well, I guess I'll go upstairs a while.

Marie (*rising and crossing to front of table*). I wish you'd stay and meet him.

Paula. Really, Mom, I'd rather not. I'm a little fed up on men just now. I'll be down later. (*She has reached the top stair as* Bill, *followed by* Tom, *enters* L.)

Bill. Say, I'm awfully sorry. They didn't have a thing that even looked like—

(Paula *has turned quickly at the sound of his voice.*)

Paula. Bill! (*She hurries down the stairs and by the time she has reached the bottom step* Bill *is across the room and has seized her outstretched hands.*)

(Marie *sits below table;* Tom *stands,* L. *of table.*)

Bill (*incredulously*). It's really you!

Paula. I thought I'd never see you again.

Bill. I've looked everywhere. And I went back to the Green Star again and again.

Paula. So did I. But you never were there.

Bill. All the time you lived right here.

Tom. Ahem! I hate to mention it, but we live here, too.

PAULA (*laughing happily*). Oh, I'm so sorry. (*The two come forward, hand in hand, to* C.) Mom —Dad—this is Bill.

MARIE. Why, how nice!

TOM. We've known Bill some half hour or so, but it's a pleasure to meet him formally. Er—got another name?

BILL (*eagerly*). Yes, sir. William Hodson Farnum. I live over at Burton. As I told you, I'm studying law. Both my parents are dead and I haven't any brothers or sisters.

TOM. Fine! Fine!

MARIE. Why, Tom!

TOM. He knows what I mean. Our name's Mason and Paula's the one we were trimming the tree for.

BILL. Paula—it's a lovely name.

PAULA (*shyly*). It's a lovely tree—and to think that you helped trim— Why, Dad! Mom! There's no star on it.

MARIE. I don't know what could have happened to the star. We must have mislaid it.

PAULA (*like a disappointed child*). Oh.

BILL (*earnestly*). Paula, it's a beautiful clear night. Come on out on the porch, and pick out a star. I can't get it for you tonight, but sometime—I promise—you'll have it for your Christmas tree. Will you come?

PAULA (*gently*). Yes, I'll come. (*As if in a world of their own, she gets her coat, he puts it around her, and they go out, rear.*)

(*The older people sit, silent.* TOM *glances at* MARIE, *then quietly reaches for his pipe and lights it. He chuckles.*)

Tom. And they didn't even know we were here.

Marie. She's gone. Our little girl's gone.

Tom. They won't stay long. It's pretty cold tonight.

Marie. I mean—she won't be the same any more.

Tom. Sure she will. She'll always be Paula.

Marie. And she came home. Our Christmas trees all through the years have done that for her, Tom. She came home.

Tom. Say! By golly!

Marie. What is it?

Tom. I was just thinking—what Christmas trees we'll have now. And dolls—games—electric trains—sleds—cowboy suits—tin soldiers—

Marie. Oh, no. Not tin soldiers! Nothing that suggests war.

Tom. Poppycock. Tin soldiers never hurt any kid. Why, I always had tin soldiers and they never did me any harm.

Marie. But they *do*. They give a child the notion war is glamorous and exciting, that— (*She stops short and laughs merrily.*) Tom Mason! What idiots we are! They're not even engaged.

Tom. Oh, I wouldn't say that. They've been out there all of three minutes and I don't think that young fellow is one to let grass grow under his feet. Oh, they're engaged all right.

Marie (*after a short silence*). Tom—

Tom (*contentedly puffing*). M-h-m?

Marie. What do you make of it?

Tom. Make of what?

Marie. You know what I mean—the vendor of Christmas trees. Who was he?

Tom (*considering*). Well, you could say he's a

harmless old fellow—a little off, but harmless—who happened along at the right time. Coincidence explains a lot of things. Or else— (*He stops, apparently permanently.*)

MARIE. Or else what? (TOM *continues to puff and regard the ceiling.*) I know what you mean: Or else he's something bigger than ourselves, somethings that walks the world on Christmas Eve, offering Christmas trees for sale to all who have the price—the price of tender memories, high courage, and shining hope. Oh, Tom, may we always have the price to buy his trees!

TOM (*intent on his own thoughts*). M-h-m. (*He removes his pipe to point it emphatically at her.*) Say! You know, I bet I could build a peach of a doll house now. I never was quite satisfied with that one I made for Paula— (*His sentence is interrupted by a*)

QUICK CURTAIN

MEET MR. C.

CHARACTERS

MR. C., *himself.*
MISS SMART, *his secretary.*
MR. SPEED, *his shipping clerk.*
MR. SNIP, *his barber.*
MR. STITCH, *his tailor.*
MR. SHORT, *his radio man.*
MISS CUTIE, *of the doll department.*
MISS POST, *of the mail department.*
MISS YUMMY, *of the candy department.*
MISS CAROL, *of the music department.*
MISS PAINT, *of the art department.*
MR. VET, *of the Eight.*
LORNA MEREDITH, *an educator.*
BARNEY BATES, *a pilot.*

SCENE: Mr. C.'s office.
TIME: Early on Christmas Eve.

(SCENE: MR. C.'s *modern and attractive office. His secretary's desk and chair are* U. C. *with a telephone and several papers.* MR. C.'s *desk is at* L. C. *A comfortable chair and lamp are* D. R. *Near the wall* D. L. *is a tall screen. Along the upstage wall is a long shelf which displays a variety of toys. On the wall here and there are signs which read:* WORLD-WIDE SERVICE, SPECIAL DELIVERY, RUSH ORDERS FILLED, *etc.*

Curtain backdrops may be used. Exits are R., to outside, and L., to other areas.)

(AT RISE OF CURTAIN: MISS SMART *is seated at her desk and the telephone rings. She is smartly dressed and it is only when you take a closer look that you see that her ears rise up to an elf-like point and her shoes are elf shoes, rolling to a point in front. As* MR. C.'s *other workers come in, you will notice the same thing.*)

MISS SMART (*on phone*). Good afternoon, Mr. C.'s office. . . . I'm sorry, he's not here at the moment. . . . (*Relaxed.*) Oh, it's you, Miss Carol. . . .

(*As she talks,* MISS POST *comes in* L. *with a bundle of letters.*)

MISS POST. Last-minute orders. (*Puts letters on* MISS SMART'S *desk.*)

MISS SMART. Hi, Miss Post! (*On phone.*) I'm sure Mr. C. will take off at the usual time. . . . Of course he'll want the bells to ring. . . . 'Bye. (*Hangs up.*)

MISS POST. The music department?

MISS SMART. She's worried about some ridiculous rumor. (*Looks at letters.*) You've classified these orders?

MISS POST. And sent a duplicate to the shipping clerk.

MISS SMART (*looking at an envelope*). Stamped "Urgent."

MISS POST. A little boy in Cleveland wants a

MEET MR. C. 95

space helmet. He says he helped his mother with the dishes.

Miss Smart. Astronaut outfits are in big demand this year.

Miss Post. Little girls want wiglets like their mothers.

(*As they talk*, Miss Cutie *comes in* L., *carrying a pretty doll.*)

Miss Cutie. Nonsense! They always want dolls. (*Stands the doll on* Mr. C.'s *desk.*) I want to show this one to Mr. C.

Miss Smart. He's busy.

Miss Cutie. A special order from a little girl in Atlanta who's never had one. (*Anxiously.*) Have you heard the rumor that's going around?

Miss Smart. Nothing to it, I'm sure.

(Mr. Vet, *who wears warm outdoor clothes, takes off his gloves as he comes in* R. *and rubs his hands.*)

Mr. Vet. Cold outside!
Miss Post. Isn't it always?
Miss Smart. Have you taken care of the Eight?
Mr. Vet. Rarin' to go. Where's Mr. C.?

(Mr. Speed *hurries in* L.)

Mr. Speed. He says he's not going!
Mr. Vet. But he told me to get out the Eight.
Mr. Speed. He's sitting in his private office reading a book.

Mr. Vet. At a time like this?

Miss Smart. What book?

Mr. Speed. It's called "Tell Children the Truth," by Lorna Meredith.

Miss Cutie. Who's she?

Mr. Speed. Mr. C. said she's a famous educator.

Miss Post. This just doesn't make sense.

Mr. Speed. We've never been late with our deliveries.

(Miss Yummy *and* Miss Paint *hurry in* L., *worried.*)

Miss Yummy. The girls in the candy kitchen are saying . . .

Miss Paint. It's all over the art department . . .

Miss Yummy. That Mr. C. has canceled his trip!

Mr. Speed. I'm afraid it's true.

(Mr. Short *comes in* L.)

Mr. Short (*to* Miss Smart). Tell Mr. C. I sent his radio message.

Miss Smart. What message?

Mr. Short. To Barney Bates, that pilot friend of his. Barney's flying back from Alaska and will make a stop here to pick up Mr. C.

Miss Smart. Where's he going with Barney?

Mr. Short. Your guess is as good as mine. (*The sound of a plane is heard. They look at each other in dismay.*) That must be Barney's plane! (*Hurries out* R. *All listen as the sound grows louder, then lessens and dies away.*)

Miss Post. Why does he need a plane?

MEET MR. C.

Mr. Vet (*offended*). What's wrong with the Eight? (*Goes out* R.)

Miss Yummy. The candy canes are all packed.

Miss Paint. We rushed to get all the painting done.

(Miss Carol *comes in* L., *upset*.)

Miss Carol. Everyone wants to know why the plane has landed.

Miss Smart. We just don't know.

Miss Carol. The whole music department is in a dither.

Miss Smart (*to* Miss Post). Try and calm them down, will you?

Miss Carol. The bells are all ready to ring.

Miss Post (*starting* L.). Come, girls. No need to get panicky. (Miss Cutie, Miss Yummy, Miss Paint *and* Miss Carol *follow her out* L.)

Mr. Speed (*pacing about*). We work all year for this, get everything ready to ship . . .

Miss Smart. And Mr. C. sits around reading a book.

Mr. Speed. I'd like to know what can be so important about that book.

(Mr. Stitch *comes in* L.)

Mr. Stitch. Is Mr. C. ready to try on his new jacket?

Miss Smart. What new jacket?

(Mr. Snip *comes in* L.)

Mr. Snip. What time does Mr. C. want me?

MR. SPEED. He had a haircut last week.

MR. SNIP. He sent word he needed me. (*Goes out* L.)

MR. STITCH. Tell him I have the new things ready. (*Goes out* L.)

MISS SMART (*puzzled*). What do you make of it all?

> (LORNA MEREDITH *comes in* R., *followed by* BARNEY BATES. *She is young and well dressed, with a fur coat over her arm.* BARNEY *wears a pilot's uniform.*)

LORNA. Barney, why do we have to stop here?

BARNEY. Mr. C.'s a good friend of mine.

LORNA. You know I'm in a hurry to get back to New York. Why else do you think I chartered your plane?

BARNEY. I'm sorry about the delay.

MR. SPEED. He usually drives the Eight.

BARNEY. Oh, this is Mr. C.'s secretary, Miss Smart. And Mr. Speed, the shipping clerk. (*Greetings are exchanged.*)

LORNA. Will you tell your Mr. C. that we'd like to be on our way as soon as possible?

MR. SPEED. I'll tell him. (*Goes out* L.)

LORNA. I've been on a lecture tour and it's quite tiring. (*Sits in easy chair.*) Besides, my little niece and nephew expect me.

BARNEY. Judy and Jim have managed without you before. Under the care of a capable nurse with —as you expressed it—no nonsense about her.

LORNA. I promised them I'd be home on Christmas Eve. A promise made to children is fully as important as a promise to adults.

MEET MR. C.

Miss Smart. The little ones will hang up their stockings and you don't want to miss the fun?

Lorna. I beg your pardon?

Barney (*to* Miss Smart). You're way off the beam.

Lorna. If you mean that they expect Santa Claus, certainly not. (*Laughs.*)

Miss Smart. O-oh.

Lorna. Will someone please tell me just where we are?

Miss Smart. You don't know?

Lorna. All I could see was snow. It might as well be the North Pole.

Barney. So it might.

Lorna. Some sort of factory, I gather?

Miss Smart. Yes.

Lorna. But way up here?

Miss Smart. This is where Mr. C. wanted it.

Lorna. A toy factory? (*Goes to look at display on shelves.*) Remarkably well done.

Miss Smart. Of course.

Lorna. Where does he get his materials?

Miss Smart. He has contacts.

Lorna. And labor?

Miss Smart. We're all glad to work for him.

Lorna. How can he ship anything?

Miss Smart. Mr. C. makes the deliveries himself.

Barney. He drives the Eight.

Lorna. A Cadillac? But it's still impossible.

Barney. When you meet Mr. C. you'll understand.

Lorna. Where *is* he?

(MR. C. *comes in* L. *He is short and plump and wears a red jacket trimmed with white fur, red pants and black boots. His hair is white and he has a full white beard. He carries a red cap and a book.*)

BARNEY. Right here!
LORNA (*staring in disbelief*). Oh, no, it's incredible!
MR. C. (*shaking hands with* BARNEY). How are you, Barney?
BARNEY. Glad to see you again, sir. You're looking great.
MR. C. You don't think I've put on a little weight? (*Pats his stomach.*)
BARNEY. On you it looks good. Mr. C., I've brought a guest. Miss Lorna Meredith, the noted educator who has been on a lecture tour.
MR. C. Lorna Meredith? So *you* wrote this book I've been reading.
LORNA (*in a faint voice*). I'm glad you like it. (*Sits down, rather shaken.*)
MR. C. I didn't say that. (*To* MISS SMART.) Did Mr. Stitch bring my new jacket?
MISS SMART. He has it ready.
MR. C. Good. I'll want my barber in a few minutes.
BARNEY. Why did you want to see me?
MR. C. (*sitting at his desk*). I hope you'll be willing to take a passenger.
BARNEY. Not *you?*
MR. C. I'm retiring as of now.
MISS SMART. Oh, Mr. C., no!
BARNEY. You can't mean it!

Mr. C. Personal reasons. I'll close the plant and say good-bye to the Eight.

Lorna. What . . . eight?

Mr. C. Dasher, Dancer, Prancer, Vixen . . . I guess everybody knows their names.

Miss Smart. Especially the children.

Mr. C. I've decided to go to Sun Village in California. A retirement area for senior citizens when they're not needed any more.

Barney. But you *are* needed!

Mr. C. Think so? (*Opens book and reads.*) "Children should at all times be told the exact truth. Consider, for instance, the fiction about Santa Claus. . . ."

Barney (*reproachfully*). Lorna!

Mr. C. (*politely*). Your book is well written.

Miss Smart (*snorting*). Ha!

Mr. C. (*reading*). "Modern children have no need for fantasy. Reality, such as man's travels to the moon, is much more exciting."

Miss Smart. Oh, is it?

Miss Lorna (*stiffly*). As an educator, I'm against telling children about a mythical character and a group of non-existent elves.

Miss Smart (*as she touches her pointed ears*). Non-existent?

Barney. You must have had a neglected childhood.

Lorna. My father was a scientist who taught me respect for facts.

Mr. C. Miss Meredith is right. I'm out of step with modern thinking.

Miss Smart. I don't believe it!

Mr. C. A good thing I read your book. I was all

set to make my yearly trip to a world that doesn't want me any more.

MISS SMART. What is the world coming to!

MR. C. (*reading*). "The Santa concept belongs to a bygone day. Granted that children like the idea of a little man and his reindeer, are we being fair when we let them *believe* this?"

MISS SMART. So that's why little Judy and Jim won't hang their stockings.

MR. C. (*rising*). Miss Meredith's book isn't the only reason I'm retiring. I've had little difficulties these past few years.

BARNEY. Such as?

MR. C. A shortage of coal to put in stockings when some of the boys and girls have been naughty. Now, oil burners and gas furnaces. (*Sighs.*)

BARNEY. I've often wondered about that pack of yours. How can it hold so much?

MR. C. Simple, my dear boy. It works on the same principle as the miraculous pitcher of Greece. Self-replenishing.

BARNEY. O-oh. And the sleigh, how do you get such speed?

MR. C. By atomic power, of course.

(MR. STITCH *comes in* L. *with a loud sports jacket over his arm and a pair of bright-colored slacks.*)

MR. STITCH. Your new outfit, Mr. C.

MR. C. (*pleased*). Ah! (*Slips off his red jacket.*)

MISS SMART. You're not going to wear . . . those things?

MR. C. Very popular in Sun Village, I understand.

MEET MR. C. 103

(Mr. Speed *comes in* L. *with a pair of open sandals.*)

Mr. Speed. The shoemaker sent me in with your new sandals.

Mr. C. Fine. (*Sits down.*) I was getting tired of boots. (Mr. Speed *takes off the boots and puts on the sandals.*)

Mr. Stitch. You won't look like the same man.

Mr. C. Have you made me some colorful sports shirts?

Mr. Stitch. And swimming trunks, yes, sir.

Mr. C. Miss Smart, will you see if you can find Mr. Snip? I need him now.

Miss Smart (*unhappily*). Yes, sir. (*Goes out* L.)

Mr. C. Speaking of Sun Village . . . (Mr. Short *comes in* L. *with a golf bag full of clubs.*) Just what I was going to ask about.

Mr. Short. Yes, sir. (*Leans golf bag against desk, sighs and goes out* L.)

Mr. C. (*selecting a club*). I'll have to improve my putting. (*Amused at himself.*) Improve? I don't know *how* to putt. (*Takes a few swings, then returns club to bag.*) First these nice new slacks. (*Takes slacks and goes behind screen* D. L.)

Barney. So your mind is really made up?

Mr. C. (*from behind screen*). Picture me out on the golf course enjoying the warm sunshine.

Barney. Then let's be practical.

Mr. C. I'm doing my best.

Barney. What are you going to do about finances?

Mr. C. Do I have to do anything?

Barney. I don't suppose you ever paid in to Social Security?

MR. C. What's that?

BARNEY. For a worker over sixty-five. You *are* over sixty-five?

MR. C. (*chuckling*). Are you kidding! (*Puts red pants over top of screen.*)

BARNEY. Maybe you could get seasonal work in one of the department stores or on a street corner.

MR. C. What kind of work?

BARNEY. Playing Santa Claus. Can you sing?

MR. C. What does singing have to do with it?

BARNEY. There's more demand for singing Santas. Like this. (*In a deep voice.*) "Jingle bells, jingle bells!" (*Laughs deeply, holding his stomach.*) Ho, ho, ho! Merry Christmas, everybody!

MR. C. (*doubtfully*). I suppose I could try.

BARNEY. There's just a chance you might qualify for unemployment compensation.

MR. C. I don't understand.

BARNEY. Simply state that your work is seasonable and apply for a nice fat check.

MR. C. Get paid for doing nothing?

BARNEY. It would give you plenty of time to play golf.

(MR. C. *comes out from behind the screen wearing both slacks and jacket.* MISS SMART *comes in* L. *and covers her eyes.*)

MR. C. Well, look at me now!

BARNEY. Quite a change. (*As* MR. C. *selects a club and starts swinging.*) Understand, I'm not sure you'd be eligible. You're American, aren't you?

MR. C. Of course.

MISS SMART. But Mr. C., in England . . .

MEET MR. C.

Mr. C. Well, you might say I'm English, too.

Miss Smart. And in Germany, and Holland, and France, and Canada . . .

Mr. C. All right, so I'm a little of all those countries. And more.

Barney. Like most Americans, a mixture. But where were you born?

Mr. C. It's a little hard to say.

Barney. Ever take out citizenship papers?

Mr. C. I never considered it necessary.

Barney. I'll have to look into your legal rights.

Mr. C. What's keeping that barber?

Miss Smart. He'll be right along.

Mr. C. (*to* Lorna). You look at me as if you don't believe your eyes.

Lorna (*half-dazed*). I . . . don't.

Miss Smart. How could you write in your book that he isn't real?

Barney. Toys appear under a million trees on Christmas morning. Stockings are full when children creep in to look.

Lorna (*rising*). None of this is really happening. (*Puts a hand to her head.*) We're still in the plane . . . flying at too high an altitude. This is only an illusion.

Barney. Then it's an illusion that makes the world happier. Mr. C., forget about her book. Stay here!

Mr. C. No, Barney.

Barney (*to* Lorna). You say Santa isn't real. What *is* reality? Something you can hold in your hand? Something you can see and touch?

Lorna. I . . . have to think.

BARNEY. Can you see love, or faith, or hope? Lorna, how blind you are!

(MR. SNIP *comes in* L., *pushing a little cart on which are his barbering tools.*)

MR. SNIP. Sorry to keep you waiting, Mr. C. Ready?

MR. C. Any time. (*Sits down and* MR. SNIP *puts a towel around his shoulders.*)

(MR. SPEED, MR. STITCH, MR. VET, MISS CUTIE, MISS POST, MISS YUMMY, MISS CAROL *and* MISS PAINT *come in quietly at* L. *and watch in dismay.*)

BARNEY. Mr. C. . . . You don't intend . . . you're going to have him . . .

MR. C. (*to* MR. SNIP). Cut off my beard! (*The others gasp.*)

MR. SNIP (*hopefully*). How about just a nice little trim?

MR. C. I want a close shave.

MR. SNIP. Yes, sir. (*Takes a large pair of scissors from his cart.*)

(MR. SHORT *hurries in* L., *carrying a piece of paper.*)

MR. SHORT. A wire just came in!

MR. C. Where from?

MR. SHORT. St. Matthew's Children's Home. They have voted you "Man of the Year."

(*The others cheer.*)

MEET MR. C.

Mr. C. (*pleased*). How good of them. (*Then shakes his head.*) But some famous educator will soon tell them there isn't any Santa.

Barney. The children may simply decide there aren't any educators.

Lorna. You mean, I'm not real?

Barney. Can you prove it?

Lorna (*slowly*). I'm beginning to understand what you mean. Lots of things can't be proved . . . like love.

Barney. That's what I've been saying.

Lorna. Santa Claus won't come to Judy and Jim because I . . . because I . . .

Barney. He won't come anywhere, ever again.

Lorna. Because of me and others like me. (*Suddenly.*) Oh, is it too late?

Barney. Ask Mr. C.

Lorna (*going to* Mr. C.). I see now that I did have a neglected childhood. There was no magic in it. (*As she talks,* Mr. C. *leans back and* Mr. Snip *raises the scissors, ready to cut the beard.*) No, stop! (Mr. Snip *lowers the scissors.*) You're *not* merely a fantasy. You're generosity and kindness. The love that people have for little children.

Mr. C. You believe in me now?

Lorna. I do, I do! Please don't retire!

Mr. C. Do you think I *wanted* to play golf? (*Jumps up.*) I'll make my trip! (*Throws off the towel and the sports jacket and* Miss Smart *helps him on with his red one. She puts the cap on his head.*)

Miss Smart. Hurry, hurry!

Mr. Speed. Your pack is in the sleigh.

Mr. Vet. The Eight are waiting.

(MISS CAROL *goes out* L.)

ALL. Good-bye! Happy landings!
MR. C. I won't forget Judy and Jim. Merry Christmas! (*Hurries out* R.)

(MISS SMART *and* MR. SPEED *each pick up a black boot and* MR. VET *picks up the red pants. They all hurry out after him except* LORNA *and* BARNEY.)

BARNEY. Incredible, did you say?
LORNA. Yes. But completely wonderful!

(*Bells begin to play a Christmas carol.*)

CURTAIN

OTHER TITLES AVAILABLE FROM BAKER'S PLAYS

4X'MAS

George Cameron Grant

Comedy/Drama/Fantasy

Four heart warming Christmas plays and one monologue play, just in time for the holiday!

THE OFFICE PARTY (2m, 1f) - Bill and Joyce meet at a holiday office party, rekindling a love affair that leads to Joyce's living room and the possible early arrival of Richard, the third side of an unresolved triangle.

SANTA'S CLARA (2m, 1f) - In the shadows of a Hell's Kitchen bottle redemption center, a fired department store Santa meets a teenage runaway toting a shopping cart of empties and a cynical heart full of nightmare-shrouded sugar plum memories. But tonight, more than bottles may get redeemed.

THE FIRST NOEL (1f) - A homeless and hungry Noel returns to the site of her childhood, now a Chinese take-out, but will her journey get her the handout she wants, or the nurturing she needs?

BALLS (4f, 1m) - A box of very eccentric, multi-colored holiday ornaments discover just how fragile their existence really is.

SANTA COMES TO THE KING DAVID (3f, 1m) - A distraught woman saves what she thinks is a bridge leaper in a Santa suit, discovering instead a story of unfulfilled dreams, unconditional devotion, a Kris Kringle who makes annual visits to a Jewish nursing home, and the crazy possibility that two broken hearts can indeed make one whole.

OTHER TITLES AVAILABLE FROM BAKER'S PLAYS

CHRISTMAS BY THE BOOK AND OTHER PLAYS

Sandra Cowsill

flexible casts range from 11-18, plus extras

This is one of the best Christmas collections we've seen. Each one-act play in this excellent collection provides a clear-cut application of the message of Christmas to contemporary problems in society, presented with humor and sympathy.

Contains:

Christmas by the Book - a stuffy hotel manager insists that her staff runs Christmas by the book, until an eccentric bunch shows her she's been reading the wrong book.

The Spirit of Christmas - a dysfunctional family learns that even the emotional wounds handed down from generation to generation can be healed.

Tapestry - examines the source of a love that reaches beyond emotion, as friends seek to help a woman who has announced her impending divorce.

Within each storyline is a re-enactment of the scriptural account of Christ's birth, as told in Luke 2.

BAKERSPLAYS.COM

OTHER TITLES AVAILABLE FROM BAKER'S PLAYS

THE MOUSE'S DISCOVERY
CHANCEL PLAYS FOR YOUNG AND OLD

Edited by John McTavish

Tomorrow We Go to Bethlehem – A Christmas Play, by Patricia Wells (5m, 4f). Through the wonder of time-warp, a group of 21st century tourists arrives in Bethlehem just as Mary and Joseph come along looking for a place to stay.

A Word with You – A Christmas Play, by Marney Heatley and Brian Martin (3m, 4f, 1 infant, real or imaginary). Simon, a shepherd, misses work one night when his wife gives birth. The same evening Jesus is born and Simon witnesses strange events leading to adventure and discovery.

The Third Wish – A Play for Christmas, by James Taylor (6m, 2f, 1 young girl or, alternatively: 3m, 5 f., 1 young girl). Three Wise Ones, called Islam, Buddhist and Hindu, remind us of the religiously pluralistic context in which the Christmas message is set.

The Mouse's Discovery, by Marion McTavish (12 children or more, m or f, except for the boys playing Joseph and Herod, and the girl playing Mary). A Christmas pageant for children of all ages featuring some very human looking mice who happen to be on the spot one night as shepherds gather, a king plots, and a special child is born.

The Good Samaritan, by Richard Coleman (1m or 1f). A pantomime based on the famous parable with people in the audience providing an echo.

The Face of Jesus, by Patricia Wells (2m). Two modern day prisoners meet on death row reminding us of Jesus and Barabbas.

BAKERSPLAYS.COM

OTHER TITLES AVAILABLE FROM BAKER'S PLAYS

THE EIGHT REINDEER MONOLOGUES

Jeff Goode

Comedy / 1f / 4m / 1m or 4f

Are you looking for something different for Christmas this year? Tired of *Christmas Carol* and *Gift of the Magi?* Well, this is the script for you: eight reindeer dishing about the real Santa. All those rumors you've heard about him and the elves? About Rudolph's little secret? About Vixen's story that was leaked to the press? All true. Yes, the reindeer finally speak up and – believe us – they do not hold back!

Please keep in mind that we do not recommend this script for high school use. This play is for adult audiences only!

The Eight has been well-received in the press:

"Wickedly Topical"
– *New York Times*

"Excellent thought provoking."
– *Dramalogue Magazine*

"Arrestingly funny."
– *Village Voice*

"Brilliant."
– *L.A. Weekly*

"Delightful."
– *Chicago Sun-Times*

"Inspired."
– *Time Out / New York*

BAKERSPLAYS.COM

OTHER TITLES AVAILABLE FROM BAKER'S PLAYS

SEVEN SANTAS

Jeff Goode

Comedy / 5m, 3f

The long-awaited follow-up to *The Eight: Reindeer Monologues*. This time, it's Santa's turn, and Christmas will never ever be the same. Scandal erupts at the North Pole when the most powerful man on Earth is sentenced to rehab for a minor traffic violation. But when he finds himself in a detox program run by the estranged Mrs. Claus, Santa's desperate struggle to conceal the truth about his arrest uncovers yet another sordid secret that could mean the end of Christmas-as-we-know-it.

www.ingramcontent.com/pod-product-compliance
Lightning Source LLC
Chambersburg PA
CBHW051454290426
44109CB00016B/1748